P9-DCP-981

The Art of
FELTMAKING

WATSON-GUPTILL ✂ CRAFTS

The Art of FELTMAKING

Basic Techniques for Making Jewelry, Miniatures, Dolls, Buttons, Wearables, Puppets, Masks, and Fine Art Pieces

Anne Einset Vickrey

WATSON-GUPTILL PUBLICATIONS/NEW YORK

Senior Editor: Candace Raney
Developmental Editor: Joy Aquilino
Edited by Sylvia Warren
Designed by Areta Buk
Graphic production by Hector Campbell
Front cover and title page photos by Tom Haynes

Copyright © 1997 by Anne Einset Vickrey

First published in 1997 by Watson-Guptill Publications,
a division of VNU Business Media, Inc., 770 Broadway, New York, NY 10003.
www.wgpub.com

Library of Congress Cataloging-in-Publication Data
Vickrey, Anne Einset.
    The art of feltmaking: basic techniques for making jewelry,
miniatures, dolls, buttons, wearables, puppets, masks, and fine art
pieces / Anne Einset Vickrey.
        p.   cm.
    Includes index.
    ISBN 0-8230-0262-4 (flexiback)
    1. Felting.   2. Felt work.   I. Title.
TT849.5.V527   1997
746'.0463—dc21   97-12773
                                                        CIP

All rights reserved. No part of this publication may be reproduced or
used in any form or by any means—graphic, electronic, or mechanical,
including photocopying, recording, taping, or information storage and
retrieval systems—without written permission of the publisher.

Manufactured in China

First printing, 1997

5 6 7 8 9 10 / 11 10 09 08 07 06

Acknowledgments

My deepest gratitude to the following people, whose contributions made this book possible:

Nina Ollikainen, for her research and wonderful illustrations;

Fe Langdon, for sharing her talent and artwork, and for making the poseable figures;

Beth Beede, for the use of her photographs taken in Mongolia;

Patricia Spark, for generously offering her artwork and technical tips, and for her support and friendship;

Becky Blackley, Ann Ducker, Bill Evitt, Nancy Longacre, and Anne Sneary, for the loan of their artwork;

Karen Livingstone, for the loan of her artwork, which was used as a background for some of the bead necklaces;

Nancy Lee, Virginia Debs, and Carol Lewis, for their help and support;

my family and friends, for their moral support;

and my children, Becky and John, for their patience and understanding, and for serving as models in this book.

Contributing Designers
Anne Einset Vickrey
Fe Langdon

Illustrator
Nina Ollikainen

Photographers
David B. Weights
Anne Einset Vickrey

Location Photographs in Mongolia
Beth and Larry Beede

Contents

Introduction

WHAT IS FELTMAKING?

When most of us think of felt, we picture either the soft, thick fabric used for craft projects or the felt boards that are popular with elementary school teachers as a storytelling aid. That type of felt is most often made of synthetic materials—usually acrylic, although there are wool and rayon blends available. In this book when we refer to *felt,* we are talking about a nonwoven fabric formed when wool fibers lock together as a result of the application of heat, moisture, and pressure or agitation. The bonding of wool fibers when they form into felt is called *felting,* and the word "felt" can be used as a noun or a verb.

Nearly everyone has had the experience of washing a pure wool sweater in the laundry and pulling it out of the dryer to find that it has shrunk to a tight, stiff material that will not return to its previous form no matter what is done to it. The wool fibers in the sweater have felted, forming a thick, solid fabric that can no longer be unraveled, even if cut with a scissors. Natural wool can felt at any stage, whether it has been spun, knitted, woven, or crocheted. In the craft of feltmaking, we take advantage of this property of wool. Beginning with unspun wool, we add hot water and a little soap and work the wool until it has bonded, forming a versatile, unique fabric that can be used in myriad ways.

This book is written for the beginner who wants to make handmade felt. It is also meant to inspire the reader as he or she becomes more experienced at feltmaking. The next few sections introduce the history and craft of feltmaking and take a look at what some modern fiber artists are doing. Chapter 1, "Getting Started: Materials and Tools," describes the unique characteristics of wool, discusses types of wool, and provides information on the essential tools for feltmaking. All of the other chapters in the book contain both descriptive material and step-by-step instructions for feltmaking projects. Chapters 2 through 5 proceed in a logical sequence, starting with the easiest feltmaking technique—rolling a simple rope—and continuing through beadmaking, creating rope-and-bead figures, and making flat pieces of felt. You can build on your understanding of the basic feltmaking techniques described in the early chapters to design a variety of projects, such as seamless felt wearables, felt masks, finger and hand puppets, and even poseable figures that can be used to make an entire felt scene.

A FELT FABLE

An ancient human, a member of a nomadic tribe, is walking on a long journey. She is wearing clothing of animal skins and has wrapped leather around her feet to protect them from the coarse gravel. She passes by some low shrubs and she sees evidence that they have been used by wild sheep. It is spring and the sheep have been rubbing against the bushes to free themselves from the woolly coats that kept them warm during the winter. Our nomad stops and picks the fluffs of fiber from the bushes and places them in a leather pouch she is carrying. The dark-colored wool is soft and slightly greasy and has the smell of the wild sheep. She sits to rest and examines the fiber. When she holds it in her hand, she feels warmth coming from the fluff of fur. She has an idea. She stuffs some of the fiber into her footwear, especially under her feet, hoping it will cushion her step. As she continues on her journey, the fibers are pressed together under the pressure of her feet. Her leather foot covering keeps the moisture inside. When she finally reaches her destination she finds that the fluffs of wool that were under her feet have become matted into a strong, soft cloth like nothing she has seen before. Can this be how felt was discovered?

FELTMAKING: AN ANCIENT CRAFT

It is impossible for us to know how and when the process of feltmaking was first discovered, but we do know that felt was probably the first textile developed by humans, discovered before weaving was developed. There are many myths about the discovery of feltmaking. One legend traces the origin to Noah's Ark: Noah lined the ark with sheep's wool to make it more comfortable, and by the time the ark had reached land the constant trampling and agitation of the animals had turned the wool into felt. A tale popular among hat makers in the United Kingdom has it that when St. Clement was fleeing from his enemies some 2,000 years ago, he put wool between

The first person to discover wool's marvelous felting properties may have been someone like this nomad, who is gathering sheep's wool to line her leather footwear.

Wild sheep. Felt clothing can be found in most parts of the world where weather conditions are extreme and where wool-bearing herd animals like sheep and goats exist.

The kepenek is a seamless felt cloak used by shepherds in the Middle East and western Asia.

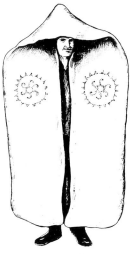

Another type of kepenek, a felt mantle.

his sandals and the soles of his feet to get relief from blisters. As St. Clement continued on his journey, perspiration, agitation, and pressure turned the makeshift blister protection into a compact fabric, which became known as felt. In fact, we know that felt has been around far longer than these charming stories suggest.

Scholars believe that feltmaking originated with nomadic peoples in Central Asia and probably spread from there west toward Hungary, then north through Europe and into Scandinavia. The best fossil evidence indicates that wild sheep evolved between 10 and 20 million years ago in the mountains of Central Asia. These sheep had hairy outer coats and softer, woolly undercoats, which were molted every spring. Their coats were black, brown, gray, or reddish, depending on what color best camouflaged them in a particular environment. Sheep were first domesticated around 12,000 years ago, and it could not have taken long for herders to discover wool's felting properties. But even before then, primitive people may have found that the wool wild sheep had molted could be felted, spun, and woven.

Textiles have a short lifetime, and so there is little archeological evidence of early feltmaking. The oldest evidence for the use of felt is in Turkey, and dates from the Neolithic period, around 8,000 years ago. There are also examples of well-preserved ancient felt from China and Siberia. In northwest China, 3,000-year-old Caucasian mummies wearing felt hats and boots have been found. In the first few decades of the twentieth century, on a high plateau in the Altai Mountains in Siberia, archeologists found graves from a group of nomadic people called the Pazyryk that contained a wealth of felt articles incorporating sophisticated animal motifs in a marvelous variety of colors, shapes, and sizes. Although the Pazyryk gravesites date back over 2,000 years, the feltmaking techniques used to make some of the items

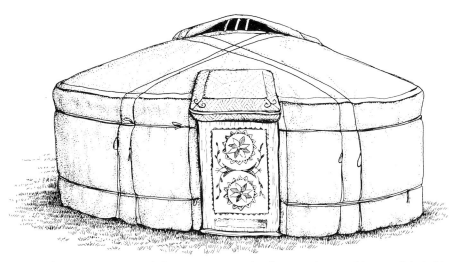

A Mongolian yurt, a tent made by covering a wooden frame with several layers of thick felt that provide effective protection from severe weather. Yurts can be packed up and moved on camels' backs.

found there are still practiced today in parts of Asia. There is evidence of felt in Scandinavia dating from the Iron Age, and the Icelandic sagas specify that felt was used for saddles.

Because felt offers good protection against harsh weather conditions, it is used for boots, hats, cloaks, mittens, and even housing. Felt has been an essential fabric in the lives of the people who have made it. It has been especially important for the survival of nomadic peoples in Asia.

Historically, feltmaking diminished in importance as societies became more industrialized, and as manufactured alternatives to felt became available. Even in recent history the craft was lost in parts of Mongolia as the population moved from the steppes and plains, which supported their nomadic lifestyle, into towns and cities. Felt clothing may have gone out of style in the Middle Ages because woven cloth seemed more comfortable and fashionable. However, one felt article that never went out of style is the felt hat, which has always been very much in fashion in industrialized societies.

Feltmaking in North America does not have a lengthy history as it does in Europe and Asia. Although some artists in the United States have been working in felt for decades, it is only since the mid-1980s that felting has really taken off, with many more craftspeople and fiber artists discovering this ancient craft. Textile artists working with felt have a high degree of freedom in creating designs because they are not restricted by the geometric structure of woven fabrics. By building up layers of fiber in many different colors, felt artists can create fluid, three-dimensional multicolored designs that are unique to the medium. The appeal of feltmaking is not limited to its versatility, however.

A richly embellished Mongolian felt carpet. Note the intricate combination of spiral and horn motifs. Photo by Beth and Larry Beede.

The designs found on ancient felt pieces from areas in South Central Asia and Mongolia incorporate animal motifs and religious imagery that are symbolic of a way of life long ago lost to us. In these high-tech, high-stress times, the craft of feltmaking offers a symbolic return to our ancient sources, to a world in which we can create beautiful art objects or wearables using only our hands and an extremely pleasant medium—wool fleece.

COMMON CENTRAL ASIAN AND MONGOLIAN FELT MOTIFS

SUN WHEELS

TREE OF LIFE

RAM'S HORNS

SAWTOOTH BORDER FORMED FROM CONNECTING TRIANGLES

WAVE

SPIRAL

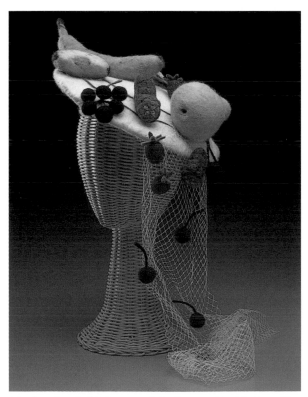

"These Boots Were Made for Dancing." Designed, felted, and finished by Anne Sneary. See Chapter 10, "Seamless Wearables," for more information.

"Daisy" felt sheep mask by Becky Blackley, The Enchanted Forest, Elkins, West Virginia. See Chapter 8, "Masks."

This handmade felt hat, entitled "She Has Too Much on Her Plate," is made with Merino wool and adorned with a stylish display of felt fruits and vegetables. Designed and felted by Patricia Spark. See Chapter 10, "Seamless Wearables."

Felt troll and gnomes. Designed and felted by Patricia Spark. See Chapter 4, "Rope-and-Bead Figures."

Marbled felt bead necklace (near right) and felt Christmas tree ornaments (far right) designed and felted by Ann Ducker. See Chapter 3, "Beads," and Chapter 6, "Felt Balls."

"Snow People" (right) and "Pasture Pals" (below) handmade felt wall hangings designed and felted by Nancy Longacre. See Chapter 5, "Flat Pieces of Felt."

Seamless coat with pockets designed and felted by Anne Einset Vickrey. See Chapter 10, "Seamless Wearables."

Scarves and mat felted from pencil roving designed and felted by Bill Evitt. See Chapter 5, "Flat Pieces of Felt."

1
Getting Started: Materials and Tools

Unlike most other crafts, the craft of feltmaking requires minimal equipment: wool, hot water, and your hands. Of course, you will need a flat work space large enough to accommodate your project—which could be as simple as a soft felt butterfly or colorful felt ball or as complex as a decorative area rug—and you will probably use soap, scissors, a scale, and a rough surface for working the felt. But all you really need to begin are hands, water, and wool.

Wool

Drawings, based on electron micrographs, of scales on a coarse wool fiber (top) and a fine wool fiber (bottom).

Wool is the most useful and versatile natural fiber known. It provides insulation against heat or cold; it can absorb a large quantity of water without feeling wet; it is extremely durable; and it is easy to clean. No synthetic material can be made that has wool's unique chemistry, or the properties responsible for the way wool fiber behaves, looks, and feels.

The surface of a wool fiber is composed of overlapping scales that, when viewed through an electron microscope, resemble the bark on a tree. These scales have a number of characteristics that affect the way a fiber looks and felts. An individual wool fiber is made up of a chain of molecules that form a spiral helix, which looks like a coiled spring and imparts the natural curl or crimp to the fiber. How fine a fiber is and how much crimp it has influence how well the fiber will felt. The ease with which a particular type of wool felts depends on its source and quality. Wool from different animals has different felting properties, and even within the same breed of sheep the ability of the wool to felt varies.

Although the marvelous transformation of wool fleece to felt is not completely understood, basically it is the result of what happens to the structure and chemistry of wool fibers as they absorb moisture and are moved around under pressure. Wool fibers absorb eight times their weight in water. As a fiber absorbs water the scales on the outside of the fiber open up, letting the water into the fiber's inner core, which is made of protein. At the same time that the fibers are absorbing water and the scales are opening, they curl backward in a rippling movement, like an accordion. This increases contact between fibers, and the spiral chains of protein molecules in the central cores of the fibers chemically bond to the cores of other fibers. As the mass of fibers is wet with hot, soapy water, the slipperiness of the soap makes it easier for the fibers to slide around, furthering the process of entanglement. Rubbing and pressing the entangled fibers increases the contact between them, and they become bonded at more and more sites on their lengths. When the wool fibers have bonded so completely that there is no more room for them to move, they form a firm felt fabric.

The magical qualities of felt are not limited to the way in which it is formed. Wet felt gives off heat, and so if you are wearing wool felt slippers and they get wet, your feet will stay warm for quite a while. Also, the fibers in a tightly felted wearable such as a hat or slipper impart to the article the ability to "remember" its shape. If you crush a felt hat, for example, it will quickly spring back to its former shape once you release the pressure.

FIBER FOR FELTMAKING

As feltmaking developed in different parts of the world, artisans used the fiber and materials that were available to them. Felt can be made from the fur or undercoat of most animals. If you have a long-haired dog that sheds an undercoat, you can mix some of its fur with wool and then try felting the combination. Angora bunny fur and goat and llama wool are also used for felting. For most of us, though, sheep's wool is the best choice.

The texture of sheep's wool varies from very coarse to very fine. Over the centuries, sheep have been bred to provide wool with various characteristics. The softest wool comes from Merino sheep, originally bred in Spain, and is used for fine articles like baby blankets and baby clothes, and for hats. Rambouillet wool, from sheep developed in France, is also used for hats. The wool from fine breeds like Merino and Rambouillet felts very well. Lincoln sheep, first bred in England, yield a much coarser wool, which can be used for rugs. Sheep that are bred for their meat, such as Suffolk and Dorset (both from England), yield a springy wool that doesn't felt as easily because the springiness prevents the fibers from coming in contact with each other. Most wool you will find in the United States is not from pure-bred sheep but from crossbreeds.

Wool can be found in many forms, from a fleece that has just been sheared off a sheep to clean wool that has been washed and dyed and processed in a commercial carding machine. For most of the projects in this book, you will use 100 percent sheep's wool that has already been carded and/or combed. If starting with raw fleece is a tempting challenge for you, follow the instructions on the next page, under "Raw Fleece." (Sources for wool are listed on page 140.)

Carded Wool. Carded wool is a random mix of fibers with most lying in the same direction. Wool is carded in different ways depending on the coarseness or fineness of the fiber and the purpose for which it is intended. Wool can be carded into large batts, for quilts and comforters, or into a pencil-thin string that will be spun into yarn. Carded wool can come off of the carding machine in a strip that is less than a yard wide. Small handfuls can be pulled off of the end of the piece to layer into a felting batt, or thin layers can be peeled off and then re-layered to form a batt.

Combed Wool. To prepare combed wool, also called *roving* or *top*, the fleece is first washed, then carded to remove vegetable matter and other impurities. After carding, the wool is combed to remove short fibers and to align the rest of the fibers in one direction along the combed top. A very thin string of carded, combed wool is called *pencil roving*.

Combed wool is easy to measure using a ruler or yardstick. In craft stores it is often sold by length with an approximate weight. The thickness of the roving can vary, so it is best to check the weight to be sure you have enough wool for your project. The wool can be fanned out lengthwise to form layers

Shearing a sheep in springtime.

(From left to right)
Carded wool, combed
wool, and pencil roving.

for felting batts. Small handfuls can be pulled off the end of the roving to layer into batts or to "fluff up" for beads or other projects.

Raw Fleece. The complete coat of wool that has been sheared from a sheep is called a *fleece*. Fleece that has not been washed or otherwise processed is called *raw fleece*. Sheep's wool comes in a variety of natural colors from whites to browns, grays, and blacks. Since the felting ability varies with the sheep breed, when you purchase wool, be sure to ask if it is good for felting. If you purchase raw fleece, it is best to wash it first before using it for feltmaking. The washed fleece will weigh about one-third less than its original weight.

To prepare raw fleece for felting, follow these steps:

1. *Wash.* Fill a basin with hot water and add some mild dishwashing detergent. The detergent is less likely to cause the fleece to felt when it is being washed than other types of soap. When the fleece is sheared from the sheep, it is in one piece. Tear off a piece that is the size of the basin. Lay it on top of the water and push it down (**photo 1**). Let the wool soak for about 10 minutes, then place your hands under the wool, carefully lift it out, and let the soapy water drain out of the fleece (**photo 2**).

2. *Rinse.* Fill the basin with clear water, the same temperature as the soapy water that you poured out, and place the wool in the water, pushing it down gently (**photo 3**). Let the soap rinse out, then lift the wool from underneath and let it drain. Fill the basin with clean water again and repeat the rinsing procedure until the rinse water becomes clear. You need to rinse all the soap out of the fleece because soap will cause the fibers to deteriorate (**photo 4**).

3. *Drain.* Take the wool out of the water and let it drain (**photo 5**). First roll the rinsed wool in a towel to blot it dry, then spread it out to dry.

4. *Fluff.* Fluff up the wool by pulling it apart.

The clean, fluffed fleece can be used for felting just as it is, to make felt ropes, beads, balls, or small felting batts.

1

2

3

4

5

DYEING THE WOOL

Dry wool can be used as is for feltmaking, or it can be dyed. You can dye the wool before or after felting. An easy way to dye wool before it is felted is to color the carded or combed wool or fleece using commercially prepared drink mixes.

1. Purchase small packets of unsweetened drink mix powders.
2. Empty a packet into a 1-quart plastic bag (preferably a zip-lock bag) and add ¼ cup water.
3. Place a length (up to 1 yard) of wool roving or an equivalent amount of carded wool or fleece into the bag and squeeze gently to saturate the wool with the dye liquid (add more water if necessary).
4. Fasten or zip the bag closed.
5. Place the bag in a sunny spot, outdoors if possible, for several hours.
6. Rinse the wool thoroughly in water and spread it out to dry.

A plastic coat hanger provides a convenient drying rack for strips of wool that have been dyed using drink mixes.

Setup and Equipment

Felt can be made just about anywhere. Sitting at a booth at a craft show I devised a way to make felt without getting my hands wet. I placed the wool, soap, and water in a zip-lock bag and worked it with my hands to make small multicolored medallions that could be used for pendants and pins. (See "Making Flat Felt in a Plastic Bag," pages 66–67, in Chapter 5.) At home I usually work next to a sink and if it is not too windy outside, I like to work outdoors on a table using a waterproof tray. Your choice of work space will depend on the nature and size of your project.

WORK SPACES

Small Projects. To make felt beads, the simplest project, you can work at a table with a top that will not be harmed by water and wet your hands with a spray bottle or small bowl of water. For small pieces of felt I use a plastic or metal marinating pan with a bumpy surface on the bottom. The extra water can be poured out into a bowl or a sink. Avoid using glass pans because they become very slippery when your hands are wet and soapy.

Larger Projects. For making larger projects, like felt wearables or a mask, you need a place to work that can get wet, and where the water will drain off of your project. Here are some examples of work spaces:
- A large tray that you can lift to drain off the water.
- A table or counter next to a sink at a height that is comfortable for standing or sitting, with rolled up towels around your work space. Use a sponge to remove water.
- A large wooden board (for example, a cutting board) next to a sink with a folded washcloth placed under one end so that the water can drain into the sink.
- A large table outdoors where you can sponge up the water or push it off the table onto the ground.

FELTMAKING TOOLS

It is possible to make felt using only wool, water, and your hands. To create the projects in this book, however, you will need additional tools, including some kind of soap, a bowl or pitcher to hold water, a spray bottle, a scale, scissors, a bumpy surface, and pieces of cotton fabric. How many of these tools you will need, and which types, will depend on your project.

Soap and Water. The main reason for using soap in feltmaking is that it makes the felting process go faster. Soap augments water's natural ability to swell the wool fibers and open the scales, which is an essential part of the bonding process. It also allows your hands to slide over the wool, facilitating the manipulative process.

- *Bar soap* is used to make beads and can be used for other projects in the book. Use a very small amount for the beads. To finish a flat piece of felt or when working on a project, wet your hands slightly, then rub bar soap on your hands and continue pressing on the felt. The combination of a lot of water and soap, which creates excessive sudsing, prevents the fibers from felting properly. Let excess water drain off of your project. Use just enough water and soap so that your hands slide easily over the felt.
- With small projects, a drop or two of *liquid dishwashing detergent* can be used to wet down the wool as you begin to work the wool. As you continue to work, use bar soap to make the fibers slide around more easily. Detergent is not as slippery as soap for felting.
- *Laundry soap powder or flakes* can be used to make the hot or warm soapy water solution required for larger projects like flat pieces of felt for masks and wearables. The recipe for a hot soap-and-water solution follows:
  1. Measure 2 quarts of hot water and dissolve $1/4$ cup of laundry soap powder or flakes completely into it. (Be sure to use soap and not detergent.)
  2. Allow the water to cool until you can just stand the heat with your hands. (When working with children, allow the water to cool to a warm temperature; it should not be hot. To bring down the temperature more quickly, you can dissolve the $1/4$ cup soap in 1 quart of hot water, then add 1 quart of cooler water.)
  3. Place the soapy water in a thermos to keep it hot, or use it from a bowl.
- To make *soap gel,* allow a soap-and-water solution of $1/4$ cup soap powder or flakes and 2 quarts water to cool until it forms a gel. Combine the gel with a small amount of hot water to wet down the wool. Then rub the wool to felt it. You will need soap gel to make the figures described in Chapter 12.

Fulling Surface. After you have worked the wool so it has started to felt, you shrink and shape it on a washboard or other bumpy surface. This is called *fulling*. Rubbing the soft felt on a bumpy surface can really cut down the time it takes to shrink and full a project. Lay the felt flat on top of the bumpy surface, add soapy water, then rub your hand over the felt. Possible bumpy surfaces include a washboard, a ridged sink drainboard, a wooden felting board, and a plastic or metal marinating pan. (For sources for metal washboards and wooden felting boards, see the Source Directory, page 140.)

Scale. A small kitchen, diet, or postage scale can be used to weigh the wool for a project.

Cotton Fabric. Smooth cotton fabric can be very useful for feltmaking. (My personal preference is for a cotton sheet that has gone through many washings and is very smooth.) You can lay a cotton square on top of a batt of wool to hold a design in place as you wet down the wool and begin to felt the piece. You can also use cotton cloth to make patterns for wearables and puppets (see page 134).

Cotton cloth can also be used in the rolling technique for making a flat piece of felt. The felt is laid out on the cotton cloth, then wrapped tightly around a dowel and rolled back and forth with the forearms for several minutes. (A detailed description of this technique is found in Chapter 5, "Flat Pieces of Felt.")

Scissors. A pair of very sharp, pointed scissors is useful for cutting down into layers of felt to reveal the layers beneath for surface design effects. Scissors are also used to cut felt ropes into beads and for cutting openings into wearables.

Sharp Blade. For adult use only! A single-edged razor blade or craft knife is used to cut through thick rolled felt and to cut a clean line to open a vessel. Cutting thick felt dulls a blade very quickly, so you will need several single-edged razor blades or a craft knife with a replaceable blade.

Towel. Many felting projects call for blotting the wet piece with a towel, which can be cloth or paper.

Basic feltmaking tools.

Fulling using a marinating pan with a bumpy surface.

2
Ropes

The easiest way to make felt into a shape that can be used in craft projects is to wet your hands and then roll and press a small amount of wool between them until it forms a rope. Thus the first basic feltmaking technique is creating felt ropes.

Making Felt Ropes

WHAT YOU'LL NEED

Carded wool fleece or roving in different colors

Warm water (in a bowl or spray bottle)

Bar soap

There are several ways to create felt ropes or solid tubes of various diameters. Felt ropes can be thin, for jewelry and small craft projects, or they can be several inches thick. Thick ropes can be cut into round shapes to be used for beads, game pieces, or pin cushions, or for combining with other shapes in craft projects. (See Chapter 3, "Beads"; Chapter 4, "Rope-and-Bead Figures"; and Chapter 7, "Small Felt Projects.") Variations on the basic rolling technique can be used to obtain more control over length, shape, and color.

ROLLING A SIMPLE ROPE

The rolling technique is an ideal way to introduce children to the craft of feltmaking. It is easy and fun, and for the simplest ropes all you need are water, wool, and your hands. As you work the wool, you will be able to feel the gradual change as the wool forms into felt. With experience, you will learn how long you need to work on a piece of wool to turn it into felt.

1. Choose wool in the colors you would like for the ropes. (For sources for wool, see the Source Directory at the end of the book.)
2. "Fluff" the wool by pulling it apart to make an airy cloud of fibers (**photo 1**). Push the fibers together into a little pile that will fit in your hand.
3. Wet your hands.
4. Roll the fluffed wool between your hands, using the same motion you would use to roll a ball of clay into a snake, that is, a simultaneous rolling and pressing motion (**photo 2**). Start your rolling gently. If you apply too much pressure at the beginning, the wool may not form into a rope shape. As you roll and press on the wool, it will turn into a stiff felt rope. If your hands feel dry as you are rolling, wet them again. The felting process is gradual, so the longer you roll, the stiffer and more felted the wool will become. A few minutes is usually all the time it takes to make a felt rope.

Making Multicolored Ropes. Fluff small amounts of two or three colors separately. Place them next to each other lengthwise. Wet your hands and roll the colors together into one felt rope.

Making Thinner Ropes. To make a thinner rope that you can use for making arms and legs for felt figures, for example, cut ropes lengthwise, wet your hands, and roll them again to felt the cut edges and make a round shape.

Making Longer Ropes. If you start with a larger piece of wool, you can use the basic rolling technique to make a longer rope.

Working with Wool Roving. Wool roving can be made into a felt rope by simply wetting your hands and rolling the roving between them. To make a thinner rope, split the roving lengthwise (**photo 3**). Place a weight on the end of the roving, wet your hands, and roll the end between them until it becomes evenly felted (**photo 4**). Don't pull on the unfelted roving as you work on it; if you do, it is likely to tear apart. Reverse the roving and work on the other end and then gradually move toward the center until you have felted the entire piece. When the entire piece is softly felted, rub bar soap on your hands to make them sticky, then roll the felted rope between them to make a harder felt.

Shown here are some of the many types of felted ropes you can make using the basic procedure and the wrapped rope technique described in the following pages.

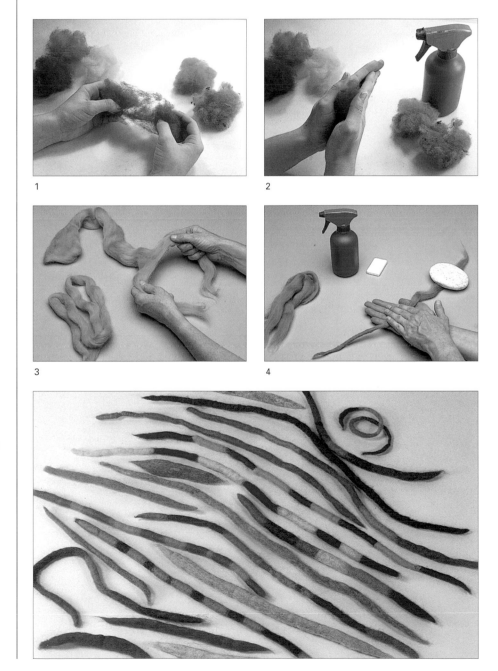

29

WHAT YOU'LL NEED

Carded wool fleece

Warm water (in a bowl or spray bottle)

Bar soap

Bamboo skewer or ⅛-inch wooden dowel

WRAPPED ROPES

By wrapping wool around a dowel or bamboo skewer you can control the color placement on the felt. The finished rope will be longer than the original skewer or dowel because the felt will stretch slightly after you slide it off the skewer or dowel and finish felting it.

1. Choose the colors of wool that you want for the rope.

2. If you are right-handed, hold the dowel (or skewer) in your left hand. With your right hand, catch a few fibers from a small piece of wool of the color you want to start with on the dowel. Hold the wool a small distance from the dowel, and turn the dowel slowly away from you. The wool will wrap around the dowel as you turn.

3. Keep turning and building up the wool on the dowel until you have about ¼ inch built up all around, for a total of a ½-inch increase to the diameter of the dowel. Cover double the length you want for the color, tapering off the thickness on the second half, which will be covered by the next color. Start the next color at the beginning of the tapered half of the previous color, and repeat the turning and winding process. Continue overlapping the colors until the dowel is covered with wool (**photo 1**).

4. Wet your hands and roll the wool and dowel between them (**photo 2**). Start gently then use more pressure as the wool begins to turn to felt. Rub some soap on your hands to help the process along. Within 3 to 5 minutes the wool will start to felt.

5. When the fibers have started to felt, cut the wool on one end carefully so you can see the end of the dowel. Hold the dowel in one hand and slide the wool off with the other hand, away from the "cut" end (**photo 3**). If it is difficult to slide the wool off of the dowel, you may have felted it too long before removing it. Let it dry completely then slide it off.

6. With the rope off of the skewer, continue to roll it between your moistened hands, using a little soap, until the rope becomes a hard felt.

1

2

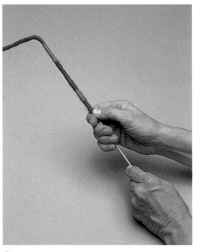

3

WHAT YOU'LL NEED

Wool fleece in dyed
and natural colors,
about 3 to 4 ounces
(3¹/₂ ounces of wool will
make a 12-inch-long,
2-inch-diameter roll)

Fleece that felts quickly
for the outside of the
roll

Hot soap-and-water
solution

Piece of cotton cloth
as long as the roll and
wide enough to wrap
around it

Sharp blade

FELT ROLLS

A very thick roll can be made of wool and felt that can be sliced after it is felted to make solid cylinders of swirling colors. The roll is made like a jelly roll. This technique works well if you use a coarser wool that felts quickly and tightly on the outside of the roll. After the roll is felted, it can be cut into pieces with a sharp blade.

1. Make a three-layer batt of a coarse wool or other wool. (For instructions on making a felt batt, see Chapter 5, "Flat Pieces of Felt," page 57.) This will be the color on the outside of the roll. Make the batt as wide as the rope you are making—about 12 inches. Make the length a few inches longer than the width.

2. Pile up multicolored dyed wool, pieces of felt and yarn on top of the batt at one end.

3. With both hands roll up the wool tightly like a jelly roll starting at the end with the pile of wool.

4. Wrap the cloth around the roll to hold it tightly in place, and tie string or yarn around it.

5. Pour hot, soapy water on the roll and squeeze it and roll it for about 15 minutes.

6. Remove the cloth and work directly on the roll. Rinse it and add more hot soapy water at intervals until the roll feels solidly felted and will not shrink any more. Then rinse the roll and allow it to dry.

7. Use a sharp blade to slice off pieces from the dry roll. The felt will dull a single-edged razor blade quickly, so you may need to use several blades to finish cutting the roll. (This step is not recommended for children.)

When the felt roll is dry, slice off pieces using a sharp blade and a sawing motion.

Firm, multicolored felt cylinders cut from rolls can be used for many different craft projects, or as game pieces or pincushions. For the checker pieces at the top of the photograph, a natural color was used for the outside layer.

3

Beads

The second basic feltmaking technique is making felt beads. Start by making round beads and tube-shaped beads. After you become comfortable with the basic beadmaking techniques, and some more advanced variations, you will be ready to create your own unique designs—both for the beads themselves and for beautiful jewelry made by stringing the beads into necklaces and bracelets.

Round Beads

Dyed wool fleece
Warm water (in a bowl
or spray bottle)
Bar soap
Towel
Scissors

Making simple beads, like making basic ropes, is easy and fun, an ideal way to introduce feltmaking to children. Even nursery school–aged children can make beads.

1. Choose your wool, fluff the wool, and make a rope. (See "Rolling a Simple Rope," page 28.)
2. Cut the rope into pieces, about as long as they are thick. They will be somewhat squarish in appearance (**photo 1**).
3. Wet your hands, then lightly rub one end of the cut piece on a bar of soap. (A little soap helps the felting process.)
4. Roll the piece around and around between your hands to form it into a round bead (**photo 2**). If you have soapsuds on your hands and bead, you are using too much soap. Wipe off the suds with a paper towel and squeeze them out of the bead, then continue to roll the bead.
5. When the bead is round and evenly felted, rinse it, blot it in a towel, and roll it again to make it round. If the bead is too fluffy, use more soap and water and keep rolling it. If the bead is oval-shaped instead of round, push the two ends to make it round.
6. Let the bead dry.

BEADMAKING TIPS

- *If the beads seem too soft,* rinse them and then let dry. (Dry felt holds its shape better than wet felt.) If they still seem too soft, wet your hands, add soap, and roll the beads again.

- *If your beads are not smooth, or seem to separate into pieces,* wrap a small amount of dry wool tightly around the bead. Then wet the dry wool with warm water and a little soap and press the dry wool onto the bead. Start rolling gently, and gradually roll harder as the new layer begins to felt to the bead.

- *If you are going to use your beads for stringing, make sure you do not felt them too much.* If the beads are too hard, a needle may not go through them easily. The more you roll the wool, the more the felt will shrink, making smaller and tougher beads.

1

2

A bounteous harvest of colorful felt beads.

Tube-Shaped Beads

WHAT YOU'LL NEED

A felt rope or ropes

Washboard or other bumpy surface

Warm water (in a bowl or spray bottle)

Bar soap

Scissors

Different shapes add interest to felt bead jewelry. You can make tube-shaped beads by felting a wool rope until it is very stiff, then cutting it into longer pieces.

1. Felt a rope until it has shrunk to the smallest possible size. (See "Rolling a Simple Rope," page 28.) You can do this by wetting the already felted rope, putting some soap on it, and rolling and pressing the rope on a washboard or other bumpy surface for about 5 minutes (**photo 1**). You can achieve the same result with your hands, if you press and roll very firmly.

2. Rinse out the soap, and squeeze the water from the rope, then roll the rope between your hands to make it straight.

3. With sharp scissors, cut the beads longer than the rope is wide (**photo 2**).

4. Roll the cut ends gently between your fingers to make them even before you string them onto yarn.

1

2

Variations

By using the basic beadmaking techniques, and mixing two or more colors of wool together or blending novelty fibers into the wool, you can make many different types of felt beads. Below and on the next page are three possible variations.

MARBLED BEADS

For a marbled look to your beads, make a multicolored rope by lightly mixing two or more colors together when you fluff the wool (**photo 1**). (See "Rolling a Simple Rope," page 28.) Felt the wool into a colored rope, then follow the instructions for beads.

TWO- OR THREE-COLOR BEADS

Fluff small amounts of two or three colors separately. Place them next to each other lengthwise. Wet your hands and roll the colors together into one felt rope (**photo 2**). (See "Rolling a Simple Rope," page 28.) Follow the instructions for round or tube-shaped beads.

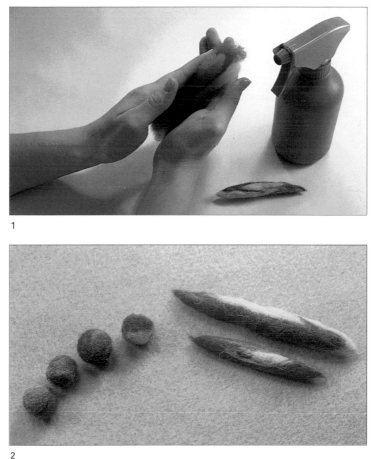

1

2

MIXED-FIBER BEADS

Use the technique described above under "Marbled Beads," but blend in small amounts of soft nonwool fibers when you fluff your wool before shaping it into a rope (**photo 3**). Experiment with different fibers and different amounts. Be sure that at least one-half of the fiber you are blending is wool or animal fur, since only those fibers will felt. Examples of fibers you can use for blending are small pieces of felt, glitter fibers, yarn pieces, silk, and angora bunny fur. After you have made your blended rope, follow the instructions for making beads (see page 34).

3

These finished necklaces show some of the lovely effects you can achieve by combining and stringing round and tube-shaped beads made with colored wool and fibers.

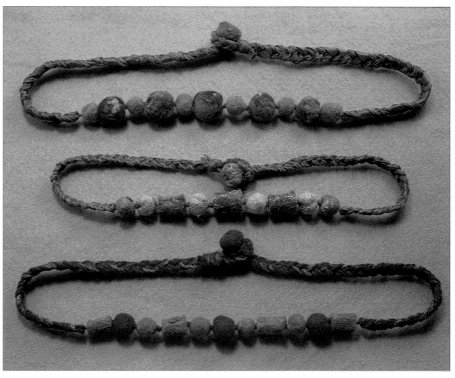

Kaleidoscope Beads

WHAT YOU'LL NEED

Wool fleece of different colors

Scraps of colored yarn, felt, and novelty fibers

Long piece of yarn

Warm water (in a bowl or spray bottle)

Dishwashing liquid or bar soap

Scissors

Zip-lock plastic bag

Washboard or other bumpy surface

Kaleidoscope beads are also multicolored beads, but they are made using a different technique from the ones described above under "Variations." With the kaleidoscope technique you can use up even the tiniest scraps of cloth and felt.

1. Choose a couple of colors of wool fleece for the background colors.
2. Collect scraps of yarn and felt as suggested above.
3. Spread out the wool in a thin layer. Place the scraps of yarn and felt in a row on top of the wool (**photo 1**), then place a thin layer of wool on top of the pile.
4. Start on one side and roll up the wool, like a jelly roll (**photo 2**).
5. Wet your hands and roll the wool gently between them so that it begins to felt (**photo 3**). (If you have too much wool to easily roll between your hands, see the instructions for making "Large Kaleidoscope Beads," page 40.)
6. When the wool starts to felt, tie a piece of yarn tightly every inch along the rope, knotting it twice, then cut the rope in the center between the ties (**photo 4**).
7. Roll each cut piece gently between your hands to make it round (**photo 5**). Wet your hands; put a little soap on the bead and roll it between your hands to felt it. The yarn tie will disappear into the bead.
8. Rinse the bead and squeeze out the water then roll it again and let it dry.

1

2

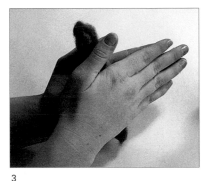

3

4

5

LARGE KALEIDOSCOPE BEADS

If you want to make large beads, you must start with a large amount of wool to make your roll. An easy way to make large felt rolls is by using a zip-lock plastic bag to start the felting process.

1. Follow the instructions on page 39 for making the jelly roll of wool and scraps of yarn and felt, but use twice as much wool and scraps. Make your roll the same length as the bottom of the plastic bag.
2. When the roll is ready, squirt about $1/4$ teaspoon liquid soap into the bag, then add 1 tablespoon of water and gently mix it with the soap.
3. Place the wool roll in the bottom of the bag (photo 1) and gently squeeze the roll to get it wet and soapy. Press the air out of the bag and squeeze the roll for 5 minutes to start felting the wool (photo 2). Next, roll the bag and wool on a washboard or bumpy surface for another three minutes. Be sure to keep the wool roll tightly in place on the bottom of the plastic bag as you work.
4. Remove the roll from the bag and continue to work on it by rolling it between your hands, or on a washboard or bumpy surface.
5. After several minutes, rinse the soap out of the roll.
6. Tie pieces of yarn tightly at intervals along the roll, then cut the roll into pieces between each tie.
7. Roll the cut pieces gently in your hands to make them round. Wet your hands, rub some soap on each bead, and roll them around and around to felt the wool. The bead will shrink a little as it continues to felt.
8. When you have felted the bead as much as you can, rinse out the soap and let it dry.

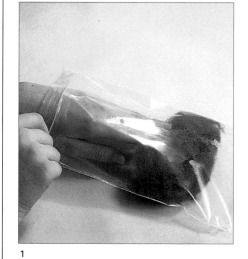

1

2

SQUARE KALEIDOSCOPE BEADS

Kaleidoscope beads reveal beautiful designs when they are cut into squares. Be sure the bead is felted very well, then cut the sides to make a square, or cut the bead in half with sharp scissors (**photo 1**). Wonderful color patterns appear in the cut areas (**photo 2**). The color combinations you can create for your felt beads are limited only by your imagination.

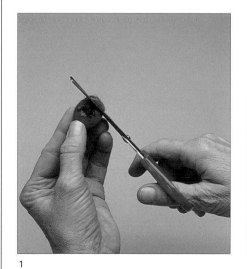

1

2

Stringing Felt Beads onto Yarn

WHAT YOU'LL NEED
Two-ply yarn
Tapestry needle
Scissors

After you have finished making your felt beads you are ready to string them for a necklace or a bracelet.

1. Cut a length of yarn or string that is a few inches longer than the necklace or bracelet you are making.

2. Lay out the beads the way you want them to be threaded. Find the middle bead and string it onto the middle of the strand of yarn. If you can't get the needle and yarn through the beads, try pushing the needle in at another spot (see photo 1).

3. Make a knot on each side of the bead to hold it in place. Thread the rest of the beads, in order, onto each side of the middle bead.

4. Hold the necklace up to figure out how long you want it. Measure the length from the last bead threaded to the end of the necklace. Cut pieces of yarn and ribbon (if desired) that are twice as long as the length you measured for one side of the necklace. Measure and cut the same combination of strands of yarn for the other side of the necklace, but make them 2 inches longer to allow for the fastening loop at the end (see step 7, below).

5. Loop a knot after the last bead, but before you tighten it, slip the strands of yarn or ribbon through the loop (**drawing 2**), then tighten the knot in the middle of the strands that you added (**drawing 3**).

6. Separate the strands into three sections and braid them to the length of necklace that you want. Make a knot at the end of the braid by knotting the whole braid and pushing the knot to the end of the braid.

7. To fasten the necklace around your neck, make a loop at the end on the longer side by folding the braid back onto itself and knotting it, or by wrapping another piece of yarn around the strands to secure the loop. Tie a knot in the braid at the other end and thread a bead onto the longer strands; make a tight knot at the end of the bead (**drawing 4**). To make it extra secure, thread the strands back through the bead and knot them. Trim the ends of the necklace, and your necklace or bracelet is finished!

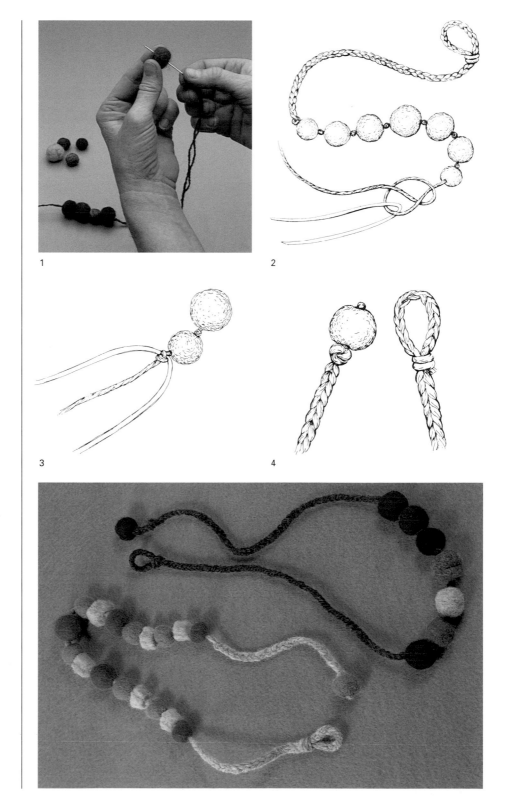

1

2

3

4

Finished necklaces strung with felt beads.

4

Rope-and-Bead Figures

Felt ropes and beads are the basic building blocks for creating felt animals, dolls that will stand up on their own, and other figures that can be used in a variety of ways: for a felt menagerie, for jewelry, and for fashion accessories.

The Basic Elements

Dyed fleece

Soap

Warm water (in bowl or spray bottle)

Towel

Scissors

Washboard or other bumpy surface

Starting with ropes and beads of different colors you can build up layers of solid colors to make many different kinds of animals. You can also use the basic elements to make dolls. After you have mastered the basics, you can go on to design your own rope-and-bead people, to make figures that will stand up on their own.

CREATING THE BASIC SHAPES

The instructions given below for making a teddy bear can be adapted for making a variety of felt figures. If you have trouble with any of the initial steps, refer to the detailed instructions for making simple ropes (pages 28–29) and beads (pages 34–36).

1. Follow the directions for making a simple rope (page 28).
2. Cut a piece from the thickest part of the rope to be the body of the bear. Cut a smaller piece from the rope to use for the head.
3. Wet your hands and rub a little soap on the pieces, then roll each piece until it forms into a round ball.

ENLARGING A BEAD

If you want to make a round bead larger (for the body of an animal, for example), first wrap dry wool around the bead as tightly as you can (**photo 1**). Wet the dry wool, add a little soap, then slowly and gently press the dry wool onto the bead. As the wool starts to felt, roll the bead around in your hands until the outside layer becomes smooth and evenly felted to the bead (**photo 2**). Add more water to your hands and soap to the bead as you are working.

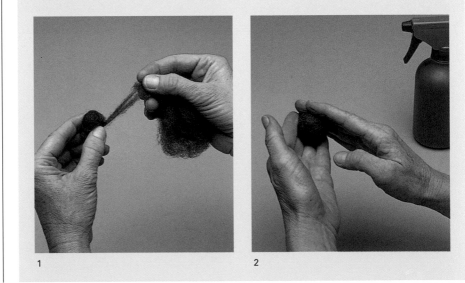

1   2

4. For the arms and legs, make a rope using the technique for tube-shaped beads, rolling it until it is well felted. Check to make sure the tube is the right size to make arms and legs that will fit on your body by holding the rope up to the body piece. If the rope is too thick, cut it lengthwise, wet your hands, and roll until the cut piece is round and evenly felted.

5. Felt the rope as much as you can by wetting it, adding soap, and rolling it between your hands. Or roll it over a washboard or other bumpy surface with as much pressure as you can.

6. Rinse all the pieces for the bear, blot them in a towel, roll them to shape them again, and let them dry.

7. Cut the rope into pieces for the bear's arms and legs. Arrange them for gluing or sewing together (**drawing 1**).

8. To make ears for the bear, trim the end pieces of the ropes into half-circle ears. If the end piece is too thick for one ear, cut it in two for two ears.

9. Glue or sew everything together but the ears. (See "Assembling the Figure," below.)

10. Place a thin line of glue along the straight edge of the ear and attach it to the head.

ASSEMBLING THE FIGURE

After you have made and arranged the felt pieces the way they should look for the finished figure, you can glue or sew the pieces together (**photo 2**). The fastest and easiest way is with a low-temperature glue gun, but you can also use craft glue or a needle and thread.

1

2

Using Craft Glue. A thick craft glue works best. Squeeze the water out of the felt pieces and let them dry. Glue one or two pieces onto the body at a time and let the glue dry before gluing on the next piece. Apply glue to the cut ends of the arms and legs that are to be attached together. After all pieces are glued, let the figure dry overnight before wrapping clothes on it or adding hair.

Using a Glue Gun. A low-temperature glue gun is preferred because you are working with small pieces and are more likely to touch the glue. Arrange the pieces and let the glue gun heat up. Start with the head: place a bead of hot glue on the top end of the body piece and attach the head. Hold the pieces together for a few seconds until the glue cools. Use the same procedure for the arms and legs (**photo 3**). Attach the ears last (**photo 4**).

Sewing. You can sew the figure together using a sewing needle and thread that will blend in with the color of the felt. Or you can use a tapestry needle and yarn in a matching color. Start at a place where the knot will be hidden between two pieces, and end the thread where the knot will be covered up (**drawing 5**). (For example, you might end at the neck, covering the knot with a yarn tie; or you might end at the head, covering the knot with hair.) Even if you are sewing together your figure, you will probably want to glue on the ears (**drawing 6**).

3

4

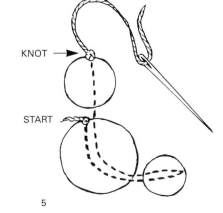

5

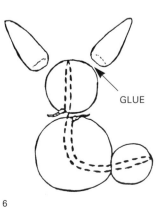

6

A felt mother duck and chicks.

Using simple basic techniques in a creative way, you can make complex figures, like this elephant and clown.

The possibilities for your menagerie are endless.

49

Rope-and-Bead People

WHAT YOU'LL NEED

Supplies for making ropes and beads (pages 28, 34, and 36)

Wool fleece, natural and colored, for skin, hair, and clothing

Pencil and paper

Glue or thread

Polymer clay (see below, under "Clay Feet")

Bar soap

Warm water

Towel

Ethnically diverse little felt people are a fun project for children. After the dolls are glued or sewn together, wool is wrapped around them for clothing, and hair is glued or sewn onto the heads.

1. With paper and pencil, roughly sketch the outline of the doll you wish to make. Note where the pieces will be glued together.

2. Make the individual using the rope-making and beadmaking techniques described on pages 28–29 and 34–36.

3. After you have felted the rope pieces as much as you can, rinse them, squeeze out the excess water, roll them to shape them, and let them dry. Cut pieces for the arms and legs to match the drawing and cut a piece for the body. The body piece can be the same size as the leg piece. As you wrap wool around the doll for clothes, the body will become larger.

4. Glue or sew the pieces together using the instructions on pages 47–48 for "Assembling the Figure."

CLOTHES

When the dolls are glued or sewn together, finish them by wrapping brightly colored wool around them for clothes.

5. Hold a small handful of wool and pull out a few fibers at a time.

6. Hold the doll in your left hand if you are right-handed (use your right hand if you are left-handed).

7. Pull out a few fibers from the wool and hold them on the doll's waist with your left thumb.

8. Turn the figure around and wrap the wool around the body (**photo 1**). Slowly pull more fibers out from the handful of wool. Keep wrapping until you have covered the doll with the right thickness of wool. Try not to wrap the wool too tightly or too loosely. The photos on the opposite page show techniques for specific types of clothing. For shirt and tops, wrap from front to back across the shoulders and under the arms on each side (**photos 2 and 3**). For trousers and long pants, wrap between the legs first, then around the waist, and down and up each leg (**photo 4**). For skirts, start at the waist and wrap around both legs loosely (**photo 5**). Wrap a contrasting color around the waist for a belt (**photo 6**). For dresses, use the same color and wrap as you would for a top and a skirt.

1

2

3

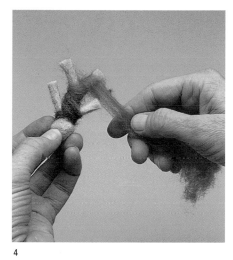

4

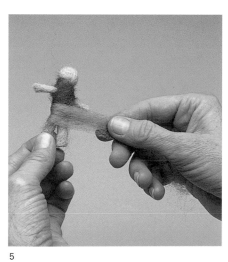

5

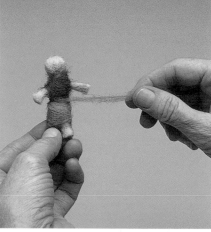

6

HAIR

After you have wrapped clothes around the doll, you can glue or sew on hair.

9. Choose a hair color and pull off enough fiber for a head of hair.

10. Arrange the fiber, adding more if you need to, then hold it up to the doll to check it. If the hair is too long, it can be cut shorter after you glue or sew it to the doll.

11. Attach the hair.

    - *Gluing on the hair.* Whether you are using craft glue or a glue gun, put a bead of glue around the head where the hair line is and some glue on top of the head (**photo 7**). Press the hair onto the head, making sure that you push it into the glue. Hold it for a few seconds if you are using a glue gun, longer for craft glue (**photo 8**).

    - *Sewing on the hair.* Choose sewing thread that is close to the hair color you chose. While you are holding the hair in place, make small stitches around the head to attach the hair (**photo 9**).

12. When the glue is dry or the sewing is completed, cut the hair to shape it, or tie the hair back with a piece of yarn or thin ribbon (**photo 10**).

7

8

9

10

CLAY FEET

After your people have been put together, you can make small clay shoes that will enable them to stand up on their own. For the shoes, use polymer clay that can be baked in the oven at a temperature too low to burn wool. (Choose clay that bakes hard at an oven temperature between 180 and 200°F.)

12. Choose a color that goes with the colors of your figure, then pinch off pieces of clay to form the shoes.

13. Use the eraser end of a pencil to make holes in the shoes, then push the legs into the holes in the clay (**photo 11**).

14. Bake the doll with shoes in the oven, following the directions for the clay. At the end of the baking time, the leg pieces will be baked into the clay. You can also bake the shoes separately and then glue them onto the finished doll.

11

A multiethnic collection of rope-and-bead dolls.

5

Flat Pieces of Felt

Making a flat piece of felt is the third basic feltmaking technique. Combining ropes and beads with flat pieces of felt allows the felter to design an almost infinite array of projects. Flat pieces can be cut and built into a variety of shapes, for flat or three-dimensional crafts. As with making beads and ropes, the crafter can design his or her own felt, incorporating an assortment of fibers and colors of wool into it.

Making Flat Pieces of Felt

WHAT YOU'LL NEED

Wool (for amounts, see box, "How Much Wool Will I Need?")

Decorative fibers (e.g., colored yarn or fur)

Piece of smooth cotton cloth (for size, see below, under "Wetting the Wool")

Washboard or other bumpy surface

Hot soap-and-water solution

Bar soap

Towel

Feltmaking is a gradual process. As you work, gently at first and then more vigorously, more and more of the wool fibers bond together to form felt. When you have worked the wool so that it holds its shape but is still somewhat fibrous, you have made *soft felt*. As you continue to work on the soft felt, adding hot, soapy water and rubbing it vigorously on a felting surface or washboard, the fibers become tighter and tighter, causing it to shrink and become more solid, creating a hard felt. The process of vigorously working soft felt to create hard felt is called *fulling*.

Throughout history and in different cultures in which feltmaking is an important industry, many methods for making flat pieces of felt have evolved. Some fiber artists start with a knitted or woven wool fabric and make felt by fulling it in a washing machine using soap and hot water. Some specific techniques for making soft felt and continuing on to full the felt are described in this section. You will use a variety of techniques to get your wool to a finished stage.

There are three basic steps in making flat pieces of felt.
1. Making a felting batt or layered pile of wool.
2. Wetting the wool.
3. Felting the wool, creating flat felt pieces that are soft, medium, or hard.

HOW MUCH WOOL WILL I NEED?

The amount of wool you will need depends on what project you will be using it for. Keep the following two guidelines in mind:

- For a piece of felt with a finished size of 5 inches square, you generally need at least $1/2$ ounce of carded wool, which you will layer into a batt that is 7 inches square—that is, *1 inch larger all around* than you want your finished piece to be.

- The number of layers you will need for your batt depends on (1) how thick the layers are and (2) whether you want your final piece to be thick or thin. Depending on the thickness you want for the finished felt, you can use two to five layers of wool for a batt. Two layers in the felting batt will be enough for a thin felt for note cards, but a thicker felt is more appropriate when making a wall hanging, framed picture, or mask.

1. MAKING A FELTING BATT

The first step in preparing the wool for making a flat piece of felt is to make a *felting batt,* which is a pile of wool that has been arranged in layers. The wool in each layer is lying cross-wise to the wool in the previous layer.

1. Make an estimate of how much wool you will need for the project you have decided on (see box, opposite, "How Much Wool Will I Need?").
2. Weigh or measure out the carded wool for your project. The wool may be in a strip or roving, or it may already be formed into a type of batt in which the fibers in the layers are mostly lying in the same direction. Carded wool is usually sold by weight.
3. Layer your batt. The way you layer your batt will depend on what form your wool is in.

Carded Wool in a Batt. Carded wool that has been formed into a batt commercially will consist of layers with fibers lying mostly in the same direction. You need to separate this batt into layers as thin as you can make them (**photo 1**), then relayer the batt, with the fibers in each layer lying crosswise to the fibers in the previous layer.

Carded and Combed Wool in a Strip or Roving. To make a layer for the felting batt, fan out the roving lengthwise or pull off small handfuls of wool from the end of the roving or strip of carded wool by grasping the end of the piece with your four fingers pressing against the palm of your hand.

1

If the hand you are using to hold the wool is too close to the end of the roving, you may find that the fibers will not pull out easily. This is because you are holding with one hand the fibers you are trying to pull out with the other (photo 2). If this happens, move your hand further from the end of the roving, just until the fibers will slide easily from the end of the roving (photo 3).

The amount of wool in each layer will vary according to how much wool you pull off the end of the roving or strip of carded wool. Thin layers that make light and airy batts give a more even felt. If your layers are very thin, you will need to increase the number of layers in your felting batts. The thicker the individual layers are, the fewer there need to be in the batt.

Lay down several handfuls in a row next to each other and continue with the next row. Overlap the handfuls of wool slightly, laying them down like shingles on a roof (photo 4). When your first layer of rows covers the space you have allotted, place the second layer on top of the first, with the fibers lying crosswise to the first layer (photo 5). Repeat for three to five layers, depending on the thickness of felt you want to end up with.

4. If desired, place a design on the top, middle, or bottom layer of your batt before you begin felting (photo 6). For instructions on incorporating designs into flat felt, see below, under "Surface Design."

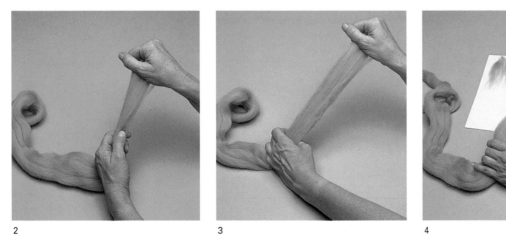

2

3

4

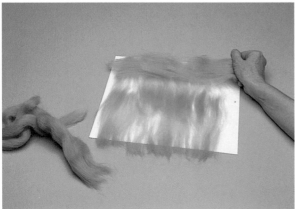

5

6

2. WETTING THE WOOL

Make sure the work space you have set up is large enough to accommodate the amount of wet wool you will be using to make your felt. Have a piece of cloth ready that is twice as large as the size of the batt you have made.

1. Make a hot soap-and-water solution (see page 24). Some wool felts more quickly with hotter water, so use water that is as hot as your hands can stand.

2. Place your cloth on a flat, wettable surface, then place your felting batt on the lower half of the cloth. Fold the cloth over the batt (**photo 7**). The cloth helps to hold the top layer of wool in place while you wet down the batt.

3. While pressing down on top of the cloth with one hand, slowly pour hot, soapy water onto the middle of the batt, wetting the wool underneath (**photo 8**).

4. If you would like a turned edge on your felt, pour water into the middle of the batt, working out from the middle to wet down the wool to 1 inch from the edge. Lift the cloth, then fold the dry wool on the outside edge back onto the wet wool and press it down (**photo 9**).

5. Add a little water at a time and press down on top of the cloth, wetting down the wool from the middle out to the edge until all of the wool is lying flat.

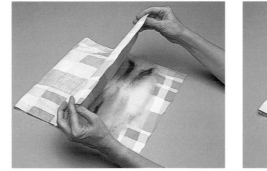

7

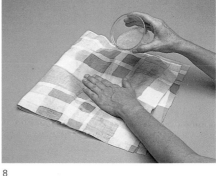

8

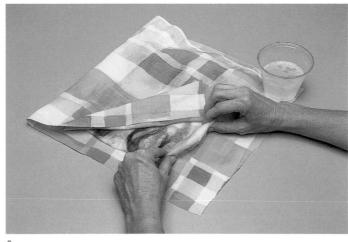

9

3. FELTING THE WOOL

With experience you will be able to identify the different stages that the felt piece goes through as you work on it. As a scattering of fibers in the piece begins to felt together to form a loose fabric, you have a soft felt. Gradually more fibers bond together, creating a medium felt that is good for many craft projects. When the felt has formed enough that you are able to rub it vigorously on a washboard or other bumpy surface without having it pull apart, you are at the fulling stage. As you full the piece on a washboard using more force, along with soap and hot water, you will finally reach a stage where you cannot make the felt shrink any more no matter how much pressure you use. This hard felt stage is at the opposite end of the spectrum from the loose fibers you began with.

Depending on what you intend to do with the felt, you can stop at the soft felt stage, or can go on to make medium or hard felt. Soft felt is suitable for some decorative pieces, medium felt for others. If you are making felt for wearables, it needs to be strong. A hard felt will give you the longest wear.

Don't give up if you think the felt is not forming quickly enough. Rinse out your project in warm water, add more soap, and continue to work on it, and it will continue to shrink. As long as you have started with wool that will felt, you just need to keep pressing and rubbing the fibers and they will eventually felt into a sturdy fabric.

Making Soft Felt

When enough of the fibers have bonded together so that the piece holds together loosely, you have made soft felt. Soft felt can be used to cut out shapes for leaves or petals, for example, and it can be felted into a batt for surface designs. After cutting out shapes from the soft felt, you can continue to felt the cut pieces.

1. Once you have wet down your felting batt inside the cotton cloth, you are ready to felt the wool. Push down all over the piece for 5 minutes (**photo 10**). Use both hands and as much pressure as you can. To exert the most pressure on the wool, you can:
   - Lean on your hands.
   - Press with one hand on top of the other.
   - Roll your hand over the wool—press first with your palm, then with your fingers.
   - Once the piece begins to flatten, hold down and press small areas for a few seconds each, moving your hand until you have pressed down on the whole piece.
2. Every once in a while as you are working, pour off the cool water and add a few tablespoons ($1/8$ cup) of hot, soapy water to the middle of the piece to keep the wool warm.
3. If the wool becomes too sudsy, pour clear warm water over it to rinse away some of the suds, then drain off the excess water.

4. The wool wrapped inside the cloth can be softly felted using a washboard or other bumpy surface. Place the cloth-wrapped felt flat on the washboard and press down on top of it, only moving your hand ¼ inch back and forth for 1 to 2 minutes, covering the whole area (**photo 11**). Turn it ¼ turn and repeat, then do the same on the other side. After working both sides in each direction one time, a soft felt will have formed.

5. Rinse out the soap, squeeze out the water, and then open the cloth and remove the soft felt.

6. When the felt is dry, cut shapes for your project.

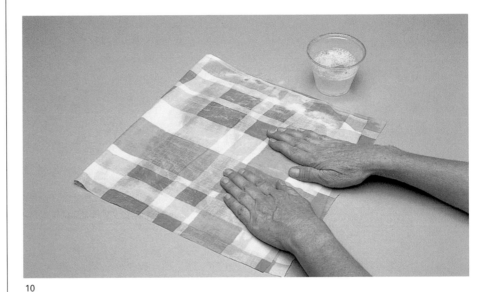

10

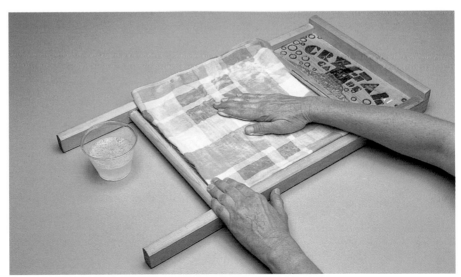

11

Felting and Fulling: Making Medium and Hard Felt

When you go on working soft felt by pressing and rubbing it, the fibers continue the bonding process. As the piece becomes stronger, you reach the second stage of the feltmaking process, fulling. The two ways to full felt are by rubbing it over a washboard, or by using the rolling technique described on pages 68–69.

1. Continue to press down on each side of the soft piece of felt for 5 minutes, using the same techniques that you used for creating the soft felt.
2. Add hot, soapy water at intervals during the felting process and pour off the cool water as you are working.
3. After working for 5 minutes on both sides, lay the wool and cloth over a washboard or other bumpy surface and press down over the cloth, moving your hand $1/4$ inch back and forth to compress the fibers, taking care not to move them outside of the $1/4$-inch radius. Work on one spot as you count to 25, for example, then move your hand and work next to it for the same amount of time. In order to achieve the same amount of shrinkage over the entire piece, you need to work on each area under your hand (about the size of your hand) for the same length of time.
4. Turn the piece one-fourth turn and work it again.
5. Turn the felt over and repeat the rubbing-and-moving process.
6. Turn the project back over to the first side, and start rubbing and pressing again, this time increasing the distance you rub from $1/4$ to $1/2$ inch. Turn it to side 2, repeating the process.
7. Repeat (this will be the third time) the rubbing and moving on both sides, increasing the radius of your rubbing circle to $3/4$ inch.
8. After repeating the process three times, open one side of the cloth and check the felt using the *pinch test,* which is an easy way to check if the wool has turned to felt. With your piece lying flat, pinch a few fibers of wool on the surface of the felt and pull up on them.
   - If only the fibers pull up without lifting the piece, you need to felt the piece longer (**photo 12**).
   - If the whole piece lifts up, the wool has felted to a medium stage and you can continue the fulling process (**photo 13**).
9. Remove the cloth and work directly on the felt. Add hot, soapy water and press and rub the felt over a washboard (**photo 14**). Start gently, gradually increasing pressure. The felt will shrink in the direction that you rub. Rub each area evenly in all directions and only move the felt back and forth $1/4$ to $1/2$ inch over the surface of the washboard.
10. At intervals, rinse out the soap and check to see if the felt is strong enough for your intended project. Check for soft or fluffy areas. If you find soft areas, wet your hands, soap them up on a bar of soap, and rub the soft spots so the whole piece will be evenly felted.
11. When the piece is finished, rinse out all of the soap, blot the piece dry by rolling it in a towel, smooth it out, and let it dry flat.

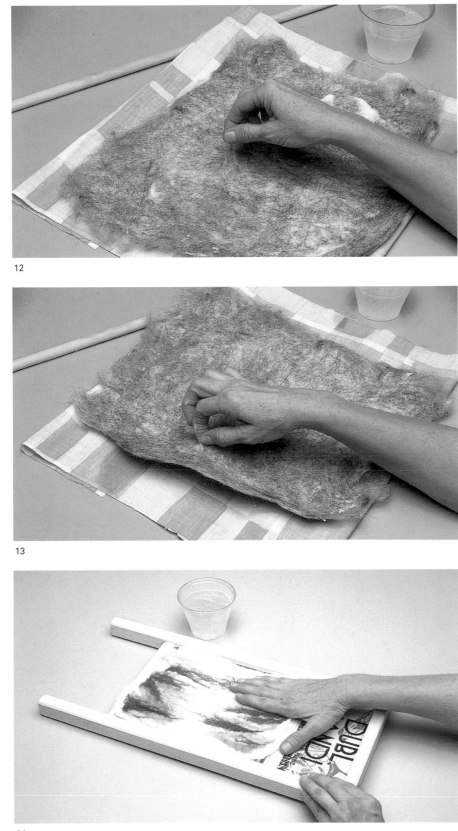

12

13

14

Finished pieces of flat felt.

Decorative flat felt pieces used for notecards.

Working with Soft-Felt Cut Shapes

Wool fleece (in different colors)

Scissors

Pencil, paper

Heavy paper for cutting template

Bar soap

Warm water

Washboard or bumpy surface

Towel

Felt flowers, leaves, and other shapes can be used to decorate hats and other craft items, or to make pins, barrettes, and jewelry. The instructions below can be used to create a variety of shapes.

1. Make a soft felt in colors for petals or different shades of green for leaves.

2. Draw a pattern on paper in the shape of petals or leaves. The pattern should be ½ inch larger than you want the finished shape to be, since the wool will shrink as you felt it. (A pattern for petals is included at the end of the book, page 135.) To make petals, you need to felt two pieces, one ½ inch smaller than the other; the smaller piece goes on top of the larger piece, to give a layered effect to the petals.)

3. Cut out the shape in heavy paper, hold the pattern on top of the soft felt and use it as a guide to cut your shape (**photo 1**).

4. Dampen the cut-out shape, rub a piece of bar soap on your hands, then rub the cut piece between your hands (**photo 2**) and a washboard or other bumpy surface to shrink and stiffen the felt (**photo 3**). Felt shrinks in the direction you rub, and so you should work the felt in a way that will achieve the desired result. (For information on how felt shrinks as you work it, see the box, "Fulling Felt for Wearables," page 112.)

5. Rinse out the soap, blot the petal or leaf in a towel, and finish the other petals and leaves in the same way. (For petals, attach the smaller piece to the larger piece, using glue or needle and thread or yarn.)

1

2

3

Felt hats decorated with cut pieces of soft felt.

Making Flat Felt in a Plastic Bag

WHAT YOU'LL NEED

Wool fleece (in
different colors)

Decorative fibers
(optional)

Zip-lock plastic bag
(size depends on how
big you want the piece
to be)

Warm water (in a bowl
or spray bottle)

Soap (liquid and/or bar)

Towel

Using a plastic bag, it is possible to make small multicolored pieces of felt, without getting your hands wet during the first felting stage, that can be used for pins, pendants, and medallions. The procedure described below for making a heart pendant can be adapted for other projects.

1. Pull off a tuft of five or more colors of wool fleece to make a small handful (photo 1).
2. Use a sandwich-size zip-lock bag and place 1 tablespoon water in the bag and a few drops of liquid soap, or place a bar of soap in the bag with the water, rub it around until the water is sudsy, then remove the piece of soap.
3. Place the wool in the bag, pushing it tightly into one corner (photo 2). Lay the bag flat; press the air out of it and seal it. Work the soapy water around with your fingers until the fibers are wet. Use just enough water to wet all of the fibers. There should be no excess liquid in the bag; all the water should be absorbed by the wool. If there is too much liquid, pour it out of the bag, then reseal it. If some of the wool is still dry, add more water (a little at a time) until all the wool is wet.
4. Place the bag on a flat surface and press down on the wool for 5 minutes. Turn the bag over during the process to work both sides.
5. After 5 minutes, carefully take the wool out of the bag and squeeze out the water over a sink. Without drying your hands or rinsing the wool, place the wool between your palms and press on it from both sides. Rub bar soap on your hands to make them slippery, then press and rub the felt between your hands to shrink it and make it firmer (photo 3). Continue this process for about 5 additional minutes.
6. After the felt has shrunk and become firm, rinse it in clear water, blot it dry by rolling it in a towel, and let it air-dry. To make a heart-shaped pendant, trim the top part of your flat, triangular piece of felt (photo 4).

MAKING A LARGE FELT PIECE IN A PLASTIC BAG

For a large felt piece that requires more wool, use a quart-size zip-lock bag to start felting the wool. Adjust the amount of water and soap; the wool fibers should absorb all of the water, and be thoroughly wet. Work the wool in the bag to a soft felt stage, then remove the wool and place it on a flat surface. Press on the piece to remove extra water, then soap your hands and rub the wool, exerting pressure until the felt has become as firm as you want it to be.

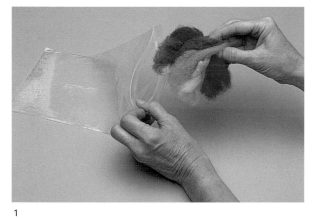

1

2

3

4

Felt stars and hearts, and a pumpkin, made using the plastic bag technique.

The Rolling Technique

WHAT YOU'LL NEED

Softly felted wool

Length of ³/₄- to 1-inch-diameter wooden dowel slightly longer than the width of the felt

Piece of cotton cloth the size of your felt

Cloth towel

The rolling technique for feltmaking described here is a variation on a method that was probably first used on the Mongolian plains thousands of years ago. In Mongolia, feltmaking starts with laying out wool on top of a piece of finished felt called the *mother felt*. Water is sprinkled over the wool, then the wool is rolled up around a thick pole and covered with dampened animal skins; the package is secured with a rope (**photo 1**). The wooden pole inside the roll is attached to ropes so it rotates when it is pulled over the ground. The ropes are tied to a camel or horse, so the animal can pull the roll until the wool has felted (**drawing 2**). After many miles, the wool for the rug turns into felt. Wool is also felted by rolling it in a mat and working it back and forth with the forearms (**photo 3**).

1. Place your piece of soft felt on a flat surface on top of a piece of cotton cloth that is slightly larger than the felt.
2. Place a wooden dowel across the felt at the end nearest you and roll up the felt and cloth tightly around the dowel (**photo 4**). Tie a piece of yarn or string around the roll (**photo 5**).
3. Pour a small amount of hot, soapy water over the roll and begin to roll the felt with your forearms. (I roll the felt over a wet towel to keep it from slipping while I'm rolling it.)

1

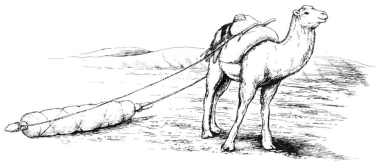

2

3

4. Place your hands together in the middle of the roll and lean toward the roll, pushing down with your forearms as you roll the felt away from you, then back toward you, in a rhythmic movement (**photos 6–8**).

5. Work it vigorously and every few minutes open up the roll; turn the felt to roll it up from the opposite side; then continue to work on it.

6. To finish: Lay the piece flat; add hot, soapy water; and rub firmly over the entire piece with your hand inside a plastic bag to smooth out the surface of the felt (**photo 9**).

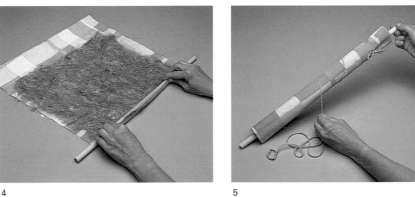

4

5

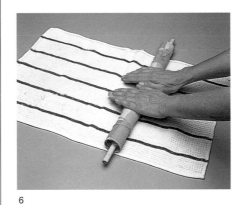

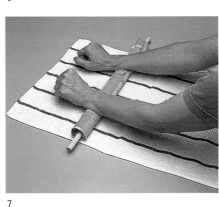

6

7

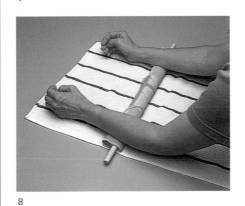

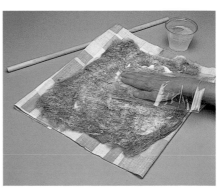

8

9

Surface Design on Felt

There are a variety of ways to felt a design into your felt piece by starting at the stage of layering the batt. Below are some techniques for adding surface design to your handmade felt.

TOP OR BOTTOM LAYER

After you have layered a felting batt, arrange different colors and textures of fibers on the top and/or bottom layer of the batt. If you are using fibers other than wool, you can help them become felted into the piece by adding a thin layer of wool over them; this laminates them to the felt. You can use one or a combination of the following techniques.

- Lay thin wisps of dyed wool on top of the batt (**photo 1**).
- Wrap some wool around your finger to make a ring and place it on the batt.
- Layer a small amount of wool, cut it into a shape, then lay it down on top of the batt (**photo 2**).
- Twist some wool into a thin yarn and lay it on the batt (**photo 3**).

1

2

3

This finished piece shows how the dyed wool changes as it felts into the batt.

CREATING YOUR DESIGN BY EXPOSING THE MIDDLE LAYERS

With this technique you will use different colors for the inside layers of your batt, then cut into and expose the colored layers according to a pattern you have designed.

1. Make templates of heavy paper to use as guides for cutting out the design shapes.
2. Layer a batt using different colors for the inside layers of wool (**photo 1**). Start with three layers of background color, then make two layers of the dyed wool, and repeat three layers of the background color.
3. Felt the batt to the soft felt stage.
4. Using sharp pointed scissors, carefully cut into the wool around the template and remove the top layer to reveal the colors beneath (**photo 2**). Or make slits in the top layer using a sharp blade, then continue to work on the piece; the cut areas will open up to show the color of the wool underneath.

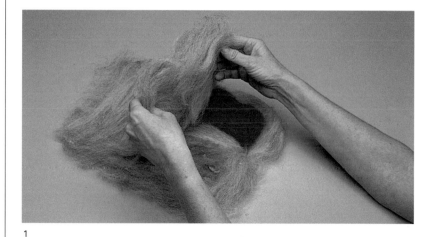

1

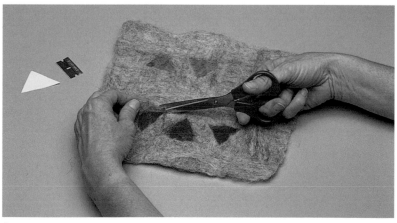

2

USING PIECES OF SOFT FELT

With this technique, as you felt the piece, the design layer and the wool batt felt together, giving you a piece of felt with a design on one side.

1. Sketch your design on a piece of paper. Make a note of the colors for each piece.
2. Cut out the pieces in soft felt. Find the middle layer of the softly felted shapes and carefully pull each of the pieces apart, so you end up with two mirror-image inlays. Place the shapes, outside side down, on your work surface, arranged as they should appear on the finished piece.
3. Place a batt of wool about three layers thick over the design. Fold over the other side of the cloth to cover the batt.
4. Wet down the wool and felt it, following the directions on pages 59–62. A cloth can be laid over the design side to prevent it from shifting during the early stages of felting.

This design of soft felt pieces is shown first arranged on top of the batt (above), then after it has been felted into the background (left).

USING THE WET INLAY METHOD

This method is similar to a technique used to make patterns on traditional felt rugs.

1. Sketch your pattern on a piece of paper (**photo 1**). You can transfer the design to a piece of cotton cloth by drawing the outline with a pencil, pen, or waterproof marker.
2. Dip small amounts of wool in a cup of hot, soapy water and lay them down over the pattern marks on the cloth pattern (**photo 2**).
3. Fill in the spaces between the design with the background color of wool using the same technique (**photo 3**).
4. Place a layered felting batt in the background color on top of the pattern, slightly larger than the pattern area (**photo 4**).
5. Wet the wool and begin to felt it.

1

2

3

4

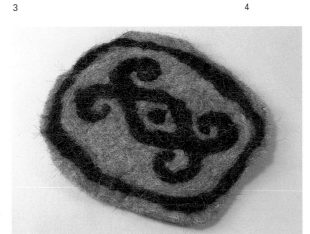

The finished wet-inlay piece.

6
Felt Balls

Making felt balls is an excellent craft project for children because the techniques are so simple and the results so beautiful. You can begin by telling the children a little about the stories of how feltmaking might have been discovered. You can even let them put a little wool in their shoes to see if it turns to felt at the end of the day. In this chapter are instructions for making felt balls in a variety of ways.

Making Felt Balls

WHAT YOU'LL NEED

$1/2$ ounce white or natural wool for each ball

Wool of various colors (about $1/4$ ounce for each child)

Hot soap-and-water solution

Towel

When these 100 percent wool balls are finished and thoroughly dry, they bounce! Felt balls are safe indoor toys.

The following instructions can be used to make felt balls for your own projects or with a group of children. If you are working with a large group of children, it is best to work outside. If you must work indoors, it is ideal to have one large sink for each group of three or four children. However, children can work over pans or buckets to avoid dripping soapy water onto the floor or table tops.

If you are making balls only the outside of which will show, use natural, undyed wool, which is less expensive than colored wool, for the inside of the balls. The amounts of wool indicated in the box at left will make $2^{1/2}$-inch-diameter balls.

1. Using the white or natural wool, pull off four handfuls of wool for each layer of a small two-layer batt (**photo 1**). The layers will be rather thin. Set your two-layer batt aside.

2. Make another 2-layer batt of colored wool for the outside of the ball. Set it aside. If you are outdoors, make sure the two batts will stay dry and not blow away.

3. Make up a hot soap-and-water solution (see page 24). (If you are working with children, make the solution with hot water, but let it cool to warm before using it.)

4. Pick up the remaining pile of white or natural wool and pull it apart into a fluffy mass of fibers.

5. Push the wool together into a loose ball of fiber that fits in one hand and dunk it in the warm, soapy water.

6. Cup your hands around the wool and move them against each other in a circular movement, shaping the wet wool into a ball. Continue this for a minute, wetting the ball again if it gets dry (**photo 2**).

7. Place the shaped, wet wool ball in the middle of the batt made of white wool and fold the sides up to completely cover the ball with the wool (**photo 3**). While holding the wool in place with one hand, splash some of the soapy water onto the ball to thoroughly wet the batt onto the ball. Press in on the ball for a couple of minutes.

8. Place the ball on top of the dyed wool batt, and repeat Step 6, wetting the batt onto the ball (**photo 4**). When all the wool has been matted onto the ball so that you have a more or less smooth surface, you are ready to felt the ball.

9. Begin felting by gently pressing in on the ball. Rotate it in your hands and press in on all areas over and over again (**photo 5**). Add more soapy water if the wool becomes dry or sticks to your hands when you pull them away from the ball.

10. In the beginning stages, the outside layer, which is thoroughly wet, will be wrinkled. After several minutes of pressing, the wool will shrink to fit the ball. At this point, gently begin to roll the ball between your hands to strengthen the felt. As it becomes stronger, roll it using more pressure. Rub bar soap on your hands and keep rolling the ball. The more you roll it, the more the felt will shrink and the smaller the ball will become. When, after rinsing, the outside layer is smooth and no longer fluffy, the ball is finished.

11. When the outside layer is tightly felted, rinse the ball in clear water, blot it dry in a towel, then roll it to reshape it and let it dry.

1

2

3

4

A collection of finished felt balls.

5

WHAT YOU'LL NEED

For each ball

1/2 ounce of natural wool

1/4 ounce of dyed wool

2 1/2-inch-long pieces of bamboo skewer (or 1/8-inch dowel)

Three 1-yard pieces of ribbon, each 1/4 inch wide

Crochet hook

Scissors

FELT BALLS WITH RIBBONS

Felt balls decorated with colorful ribbons running through them make great party favors. To make a felt ball with ribbons, you basically follow the technique outlined on pages 76–77, with a few variations.

1. Make two small batts, one with natural wool and one with dyed wool.

2. Fluff up the rest of the natural wool and divide it into two equal piles.

3. Cut off a 2 1/2-inch piece from a bamboo skewer or dowel. Hold half of the white wool in one hand, place the stick on top of it, then place the other half of the wool on top (**photo 1**). Hold the wool in place with both hands as you dunk the wool in soapy water.

4. Follow the steps for making a felt ball, starting at Step 6 on page 76. Make sure the ball is completely dry before you go on to Step 5 below.

5. Squeeze the ball to find the two ends of the stick. Push on one end of the stick so it pokes out. With sharp scissors, snip the fibers from the end of the stick. Do the same on the other side (**photo 2**).

6. Have your ribbons and crochet hook ready and push the stick out of the ball. Push the crochet hook through the ball so it comes out on the opposite side. Hook the ribbons onto the end of the crochet hook (**photo 3**), then pull them back through the ball so that the ball is centered on the length of the ribbons (**photo 4**).

7. Tie a knot in the ribbons on each side of the ball to hold them in place (**photo 5**). You can make the ribbons more permanent by gluing them inside the ball with a little craft glue. Squeeze a drop of glue into the opening on each side of the ball, then let dry.

1

2

3

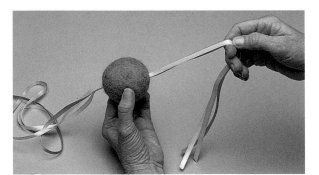

4

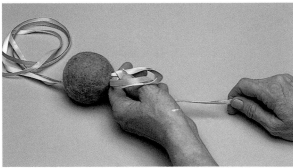

5

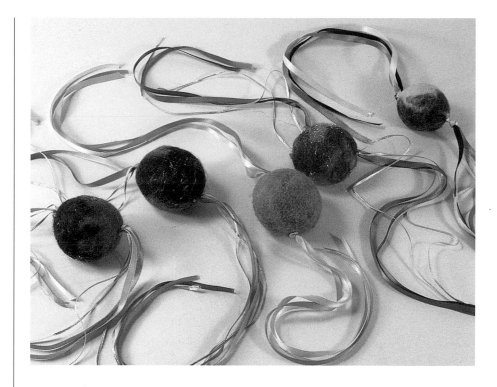

Perfect party favors: felt balls strung with brightly colored ribbons.

LAYERED BALLS

To create a ball of multicolored layers, set out piles of wool, starting with a small pile of the color you want closest to the center and making the piles progressively larger (**photo 1**). Work each layer until it is softly felted before adding the next color. Making a multicolored ball takes longer than making the basic felt ball described above, but the result is well worth the effort.

Slicing open multicolored balls reveals their many layers of color. The example shown on the left in **photo 2** was created to illustrate the many shells, or zones, of the earth's interior.

1

2

7
Small Felt Projects

Beads, ropes, and flat pieces of felt can be combined to create buttons, pins, jewelry, embellishment for clothing, or hair adornments. This chapter gives instructions for making a number of different felt creations.

Flower Buttons

WHAT YOU'LL NEED

Wool in flower colors (bright colors and a little yellow for the flower center)

1/3 cup measure (1/4 cup for small children)

Bar soap

Liquid soap

Warm water

The procedure described below for making button-type flowers can also be used for making functional buttons. Making flower buttons is a fun project for young children.

1. Pinch off small tufts of wool in colors for the petals and center of the flower (photo 1).
2. Pour 1 teaspoon warm water into the 1/3 cup measure and add a few drops of liquid soap.
3. Arrange the tufts into a flower. Holding them together, place them in the bottom of the 1/3 cup measure (photo 2).
4. Press the wool down so it all gets wet. If necessary, add a few more drops of water to completely wet the wool. Keep pressing the wool for at least a minute.
5. Take the wool out of the cup and place it flat in the palm of one hand. Press with the other hand to squeeze out the soapy water. Soap your hands with bar soap and press the felt between them, rubbing clockwise in a circular motion for another minute until the flower shrinks into an even round form (photo 3).
6. Keep the flower in the round button shape, or make petals by snipping 1/4 inch into the felt in four places and rounding the corners (photo 4). This makes a flower with more distinct petals.
7. Rinse the flower and let it dry flat.

1

2

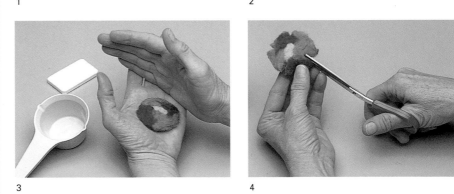

3

4

Making a Flower Arrangement

WHAT YOU'LL NEED

Felt flowers
Pipe cleaners
Glue gun or craft glue
Flat green felt
Green fleece
Small terra-cotta pot

Felt flowers can be glued into a small pot to make a unique arrangement.

1. Make a stem for the flower by wrapping green wool evenly around a pipe cleaner (**photo 1**). This wool does not require felting.
2. With a glue gun or craft glue, place a ball of glue in the center of the back of the flower. Push one end of the wool-wrapped pipe cleaner into the glue and hold it there until the glue hardens. (If you are using craft glue, let it dry for a few hours before continuing.)
3. Bend a $1/2$-inch section at the bottom of the pipe cleaner at a right angle, place glue on the short section, and glue the flower into a small pot (**photo 2**).
4. Make a flat piece of green felt and cut out leaf shapes. Place a $1/4$-inch to $1/2$-inch line of glue at the bottom of the leaf where it will attach to the stem. Glue the leaves onto the sides of the stems near the top of the pot.
5. Complete your flower arrangement by filling in the spaces between the stems with fluffy green dyed fleece (**photo 3**).

1

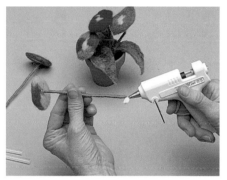

2

3

Combining Feltmaking Techniques

There is no limit to the designs you can create using beads, ropes, and flat pieces of felt. Below are just a few examples of the unique versatility of handmade felt.

BEADS AND ROPES
Combine felt beads with antique coins to make a coat clasp. Make a loop with a felt rope to match the coat material (photo 1).

BEADS AND STACKED FLAT FELT SHAPES
Beautiful buttons and embellishments can be made by cutting, stacking, and stitching together beads and hard, flat felt in several colors (photo 2).
1. Felt several different colors of wool to a hard felt stage.
2. Cut the shapes you want and stack them on top of each other.
3. Stitch the felt pieces together for buttons or embellishment on garments.

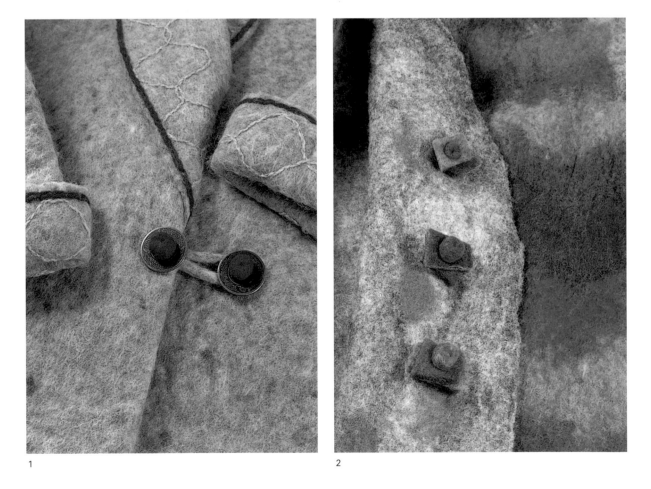

1

2

STITCHED BEAD BUTTONS

You can make unusual buttons by stitching single beads, and then stitching several of the stitched beads together (photo 3).

1. Choose several colors of wool to match your project or use a contrasting color.
2. Wet your hands and rub a little soap on them, then roll the wool around and around to make a knobby ball.
3. Stitch yarn through the middle and around four sides to hold the bead together.
4. Stitch several beads together using yarn to make a button.

SPIRAL BUTTONS

Rolled spirals can be used as earrings (see instructions on page 86) or buttons (photo 4).

1. Form a felt rope into a spiral.
2. Cut a piece of heavy cardboard for backing, and glue the spiral onto the backing.
3. When the glue is dry, trim the edge of the cardboard, then cover the back with a piece of thin craft felt or your own handmade felt.
4. Stitch a loop onto the back of the button to secure it to clothing.

3   4

EARRINGS

Earrings are made by combining felt beads that are cut in half with rope pieces and braided yarn. The earrings are glued to a flat piece of felt, then glued onto earring backings (**photo 5**).

BEAD-AND-SPIRAL BUTTONS

Combine spirals and beads to make lovely earrings, buttons, or pins (**photo 5**). Start with a felt bead and wrap a rope around it to form a spiral. Then follow Steps 2 through 4 under "Spiral Buttons," page 85.

BEADS AND FLAT PIECES OF FELT

Felt bead grapes and flat felt leaves adorn the painted wooden box shown in photo 6.

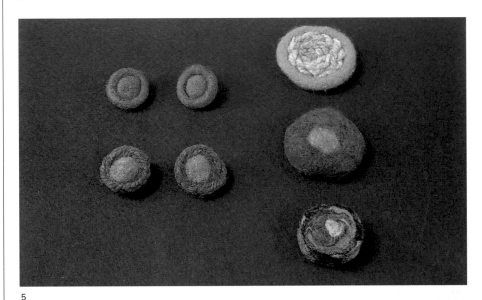

5

6

Butterflies

WHAT YOU'LL NEED

Wool for flat felt for wings and rope for body

Butterfly pattern (page 136)

Pencil and paper

Hot soap-and-water solution

Sewing needle and thread

To make a colorful felt butterfly, complete with antennae, you combine rope and flat felt techniques.

WINGS

1. Make a pattern of the wings of a butterfly. (A simple pattern for butterfly wings is on page 136.)
2. Make a 4-inch by 8-inch rectangular felting batt using three thin layers of wool of different colors.
3. Felt the wool to a medium to hard stage.
4. Following your pattern, cut out the wings in the felted wool (**photo 1**).

BODY

5. Make a felt rope. (Use Steps 1 through 4, under "Rolling a Simple Rope," page 28.)
6. To make the butterfly antennae, cut a ¹/₂-inch to 1-inch slit at one end of the rope (**photo 2**).
7. Place the body on top of the wings, wrap the wings two-thirds of the way up the body, and sew the body and wings together using a sewing needle and thread that matches the body color (**photo 3**).

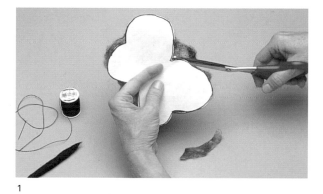

1

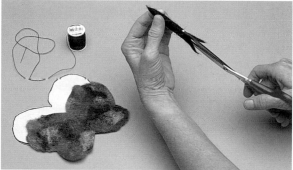

2

3

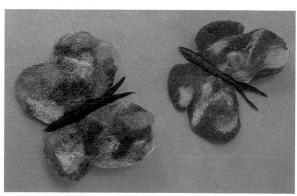

Finished butterflies.

8

Masks

The techniques for making a flat piece of felt, in which layers of wool are built up in different colors, patterns, and designs, can be used to make masks. The masks are beautiful pieces of art that are appropriate for hanging on the wall or using in plays or at Halloween. The simplest masks to make are eye masks (half masks that reach to just below the eyes), but your mask design can be as elaborate as your imagination allows. Using resist techniques, you can make three-dimensional noses, mouths that open, and even eyelids.

Eye Masks

1/4 to 1/2 ounce wool in sun colors (yellows, oranges, and golds)

1/2 ounce wool in a muted background color

Hot soap-and-water solution

Smooth cotton cloth twice as big as the mask

Scissors

Washboard or other bumpy surface

Paper (for pattern), pencil, ruler

Towel

Making a simple sun mask is a good general introduction to mask making. The process of felting the sun mask can take 20 minutes or more, but once you have wet down the wool, you can stop and come back to your project at any time.

LAYERING THE BATT

1. Measure a rectangle 7 by 10 inches on a piece of paper. This will be your guide when you are layering the batt.
2. Hold the paper up to your face and press gently at the middle of each eye. Mark that spot on the paper pattern and cut eyes in the pattern. (You will use this pattern as a guide when it is time to cut eyes into the mask.)
3. Measure a total of 3/4 to 1 ounce of wool.
4. Layer a batt of wool as described on page 57. Start by layering the 1/2 ounce of the muted colors over the pattern.
5. On top, place the bright sun colors that you want on the outside of the mask. Arrange the top layer so the fibers radiate out from the center of the batt (**photo 1**).

WETTING THE WOOL

6. Place the pile of wool on one side of your piece of cloth. Prepare the hot soap-and-water solution (see page 24).
7. Fold the other side of the cloth over the wool, sandwiching the batt inside.
8. While pressing down over the cloth with one hand, pour soapy water over the cloth, about 1/4 cup at a time, and wet down the wool between the cloth so that it lies flat.

FELTING THE WOOL

If necessary, refer to the section on flat pieces of felt (pages 60–62).

9. Push straight down over the entire cloth for 5 minutes, then turn the cloth and mask over and work another 5 minutes on the other side. Add hot, soapy water to the middle of the mask at intervals to keep the wool warm, and pour off the cool water as you are working.
10. After working each side for 5 minutes, the felt should be formed enough so that you can continue the felting process by pressing the wool over a washboard or bumpy surface, following Steps 11, 12, and 13. If you don't have a washboard, you can continue to felt the mask by hand until it seems hard enough for a final rinse and test (Step 14).
11. Place the cloth and wool flat on top of the washboard.
12. Add more hot, soapy water to the piece, and press the mask flat against the ridges, moving it about 1/4 inch back and forth. Work evenly over the entire surface of the mask in one direction, then turn the mask 90 degrees and repeat.

13. Turn the mask over and repeat the same process on the opposite side.
14. Rinse the cloth and mask. Lay the mask on a flat surface and pick up the top cloth to check the felt. It should be felted enough so that the fibers do not pull up off of the mask. (See the pinch test section, page 62.)
15. If the mask needs more felting, add warm, soapy water and continue pressing on it or rubbing it on the washboard.
16. Remove the cloth and with sharp scissors, cut into the felt as shown. Make the rays at least 1 inch wide (**photo 2**).
17. Felt the cut edges of the sun rays. Lay the mask on a flat surface, or on top of the washboard. Rub the rays gently at first across the ridges of the washboard or rub with your hands across the cut rays. Continue felting the wool, rubbing and pressing over the entire mask (**photo 3**). (The felted sun rays will be floppy as long as they are wet but will spread out nicely when they dry.) Continue rubbing and pressing until the mask is well felted. Rinse and blot the mask in a towel.

1

2

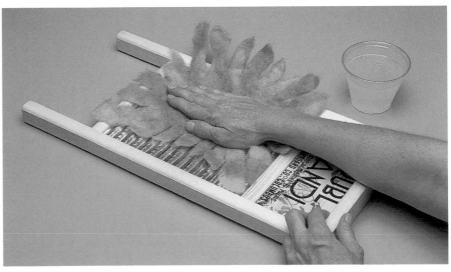

3

MAKING THE EYES

When the mask is nicely felted, you are ready to cut eye holes.

18. Lay the paper pattern on top of the mask and mark where the eyes will be (photo 4).

19. Fold the mask at that spot and make a small half-circle cut with sharp scissors for each eye. The cut you make should be smaller than the finished eye opening you want.

20. Lay the mask flat, pour hot, soapy water on the eye area, and rub across the cut edges moving it over the washboard. As you rub, the eye holes will open up (photo 5).

21. Rinse the mask and blot it in a towel. Check to make sure the eye holes are large enough. You can trim away any stray fibers with scissors.

ATTACHING TIES

22. To make the mask ready to wear, make two yarn ties following the instructions given on the opposite page. Attach the ties to the back of the mask, on the outside corner of each eye hole.

4

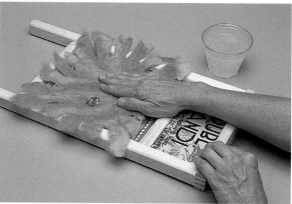

5

A finished sun mask.

Making Ties

Follow the steps below to make ties that you can use for masks, slippers, hats, and pouches.

1. Measure out your yarn. For each tie you will need three pieces of yarn.
   - *Mask ties.* Measure six pieces of yarn, each 48 inches long, matched to the color of the mask.
   - *Hat ties.* Measure six pieces of yarn, each 24 inches long.
   - *Slipper cords.* For cords that can be used around the opening of slippers (see the photo on page 114 for examples of slippers with ties), measure six pieces, each 48 inches long.
   - *Pouch strap.* Measure three pieces of yarn, each 48 inches long.
2. Take three pieces of yarn and lay them side by side (**photo 1**).
3. Hold the yarn with one hand at each end. (If you are making a long tie, you can ask a friend to hold the other end for the next few steps.)
4. Holding one end still, twist the yarn clockwise with your other hand until it is as tightly twisted as you can get it without having the yarn begin to buckle (**photo 2**).
5. Still holding onto the two ends of the tightly twisted yarn, bring your hands together. Beginning at the middle, the twisted yarn will double-twist in on itself, forming the final, sturdy multiple twisted tie (**photo 3**).
6. Make a knot where the cut ends come together.
7. If you are working on ties for a mask, hat, or slippers, make your second tie.

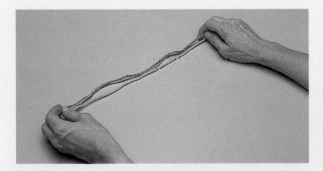

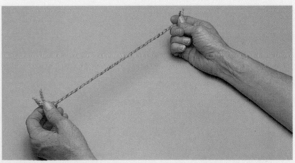

Ties are attached to the back of the mask at the outer corners of the eye holes.

Large Face Masks

WHAT YOU'LL NEED

Piece of cloth that will cover felted mask

Hot soap-and-water solution

Washboard or other bumpy surface

1 to 1 1/2 ounces of background color of wool

1/2 to 1 ounce of wool in various colors for features

Towel

A larger face mask is made using more wool arranged on a larger batt. Animal masks can be made by layering wool fibers in a face design. Look closely at photographs of animals and note the colors on their faces and the variations of color on their fur. Collect wool fiber in the various colors to layer onto a felting batt for an animal mask. As you layer the batt, you can combine colors in a way that will produce realistic looking animal fur.

BASIC PROCEDURE FOR MAKING LARGE MASKS

1. Decide what size you want your finished mask to be. Then make a paper pattern:
   - For a mask that is intended to be worn, estimate the size of the face and cut out a pattern about 2 inches larger all around than the estimated size.
   - If you intend for the mask to be a wall hanging, you may want to make it much larger than life size.
2. Layer a batt using 1 to 1 1/2 ounces of the background color wool. You should use six or more layers of wool for your batt. (See the instructions for layering a batt, pages 57–58.)
3. Cover your pattern, with the wool extending out 2 inches from the edge of the pattern.
4. Design the face on the top layer of the batt. To add detail to the mask and make it look real, you can add small wisps of wool in contrasting colors to the background wool. (Refer to the section on surface design on felt, pages 70–73, for information on how to achieve different effects at the batt stage.)

A full face bear mask.

ADDING FEATURES

5. Add the features that you desire. Below are some ideas for eyes, ears, mouth, nose, and whiskers.

Eyes. Eyes give character to your mask, especially when you include eyelids. Eye parts you can make include:

- An oval of white the size of the eye
- A circle of color for the iris
- A tiny circle of black for the pupil
- A patch of the background color of wool for the eyelid (**photo 1**)

   Cut shapes from a pile of two layers of wool in the shapes for the white of the eye and the iris. Place them on the mask, then place a tiny dot of black wool for the pupil on top. Cut out a piece of plastic or resist material and place it on top of the eye. Place the patch of wool for the eyelid on top of the resist material (**photo 2**).

1

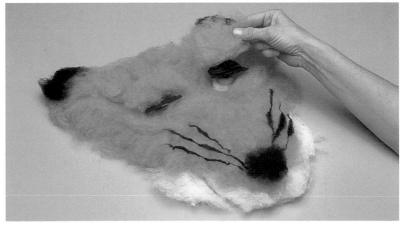

2

Ears. With the remaining background wool make a pair of ears. The batt for the ears should be four to six layers. Place them at the appropriate spot on the main batt (for example, at the top edges of the batt for animal ears, or at the sides of the batt wherever you want them to go). If you want pink to show inside the ears, place pink wool on top of the ears.

Nose. For a black nose, make three layers of black wool, cut out a triangle for the nose, and place it on top of the batt where you want it to go.

Whiskers. Twist some white and/or black wool into string for whiskers. Place on top of the pile in the appropriate spot.

Three-Dimensional Features. You can make three-dimensional eyebrows, noses, and mouths that will give a layered look and character to your mask by placing small pieces cut from a plastic bag or smooth cotton cloth between two small piles of wool to prevent them from felting together (**photo 3**). These pockets will felt along with the rest of the mask. After felting, remove the plastic and stuff the pockets with carded wool to make them three-dimensional.

Three-dimensional features can also be added after a mask has been felted and is completely dry. For example, the snout of an animal mask can be made by stitching a loose tuck in the back of the mask (**photo 4**).

FINISHING THE MASK

6. Remove the paper pattern from under the pile of wool. Wet the cloth and place it carefully on top of the batt. (The cloth should be larger than the mask so that it covers the wool.) While you are felting the mask, keep the cloth on the wool to support it before it turns to felt. This prevents the features you placed on the top layer from moving around.

7. Press straight down into the middle of the wool and pour hot, soapy water over your hand as you are holding the wool down. Work from the middle to the outside, pressing down the wool and pouring the soapy water over it so it all lies flat.

8. Felt the mask. (Refer to the instructions for making a flat piece of felt, pages 60–62.) Take your time and work on the mask for at least 20 minutes before picking up the cloth and checking the felt.

9. Slowly pick up the cloth from the front of the mask. If any of the wool lifts up from the mask, replace the cloth and continue to press down on the wool or press and rub it on a washboard for another 10 minutes. Check at intervals to see how the felt is forming.

10. When the top layer is felted, remove the cloth and work directly on the felt. Work on the back of the mask first, then turn it over and work the front, gently at first. Gradually increase pressure until the wool seems felted and all of the features are adhering together.

11. When the felt is strong, dunk the mask in water and check for soft areas that need more work.

12. Rinse the finished mask and let it dry.

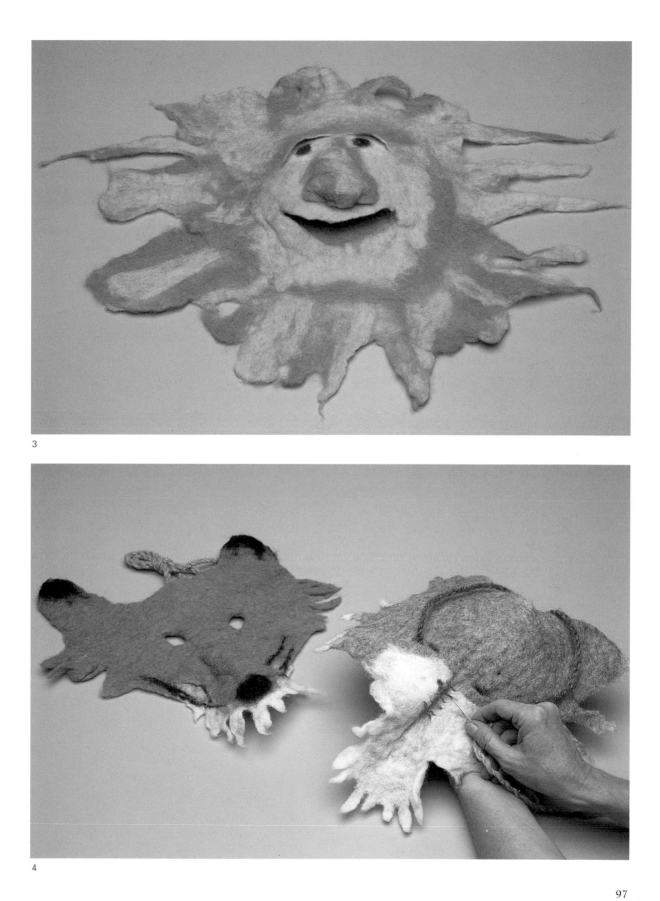

3

4

9
Felt Vessels

You can make three-dimensional seamless pieces of
fiber art by covering an object—a stone, box, or hard
plastic shape—with wool, then felting the wool so it
shrinks tightly around the object. You then cut the felt
and remove the object. You are left with a vessel or
container in the shape of the object you started with.

You can make pouches for necklaces or small purses
by felting around small, smooth stones. Jewelry boxes
can be made around blocks of wood or small plastic
boxes. Styrofoam eggs or balls can be wrapped in plastic
wrap, then wool can be felted around them. Look around
for other solid objects around which felt can be molded.
If you felt around a very heavy stone, you may decide
to leave the felt on the stone and use it as a paperweight.

Creating a Basic Vessel

WHAT YOU'LL NEED

Small stone about 3 inches long

Wool, yarn, and other fibers in the colors you want for the vessel

Smooth cotton cloth (to wrap around the stone and wool, with enough extra for grasping)

Hot soap-and-water solution

Bowl (for dipping stone into solution)

Washboard or other bumpy surface

Scissors

Yarn for tying wool (or wool and cloth) around stone

Towel

Sharp blade

A good introduction to creating felt vessels is to felt wool around a small stone. Starting with a stone about 3 inches long, cover the stone with at least three layers of wool. The more layers you use, the thicker the vessel will be. The first layer will be the inside of the vessel and the last layer will be the outside of the vessel. The colors of the layers between will show at the cut edges of the opening.

1. Choose the colors you want on the inside and outside of the vessel.
2. Wet the stone by dipping it in water, then wrap wool around the stone starting with the color that you want on the inside of the vessel. There are two ways to cover the stone.
   - *Using wool roving,* wrap wool around the stone by gently pulling the wool out as you wrap to make thin layers around the stone. Wrap first in one direction, then wrap the next layer crosswise to the first layer (**photo 1**). Try to cover the stone completely and evenly.
   - *Using carded wool or roving,* follow the technique for making a layered felt ball. Layer several piles of wool and cover the stone with one layer at a time (**photo 2**).

   Continue wrapping with the other colors until you have at least three to four layers of wool around the stone. Use the color you want on the outside of the vessel as the last color to wrap around the stone.
3. When the stone is completely covered with wool, you can tie a piece of yarn around it to hold the wool in place (**photo 3**), you can wrap a square of cloth around the stone to hold the wool (**photo 4**), or you can hold the wool in place with your hands.
   - If you tie yarn around the stone, the yarn will felt onto the surface of the vessel. Dunk the tied stone in hot, soapy water to wet it completely, then squeeze the stone for about 5 minutes.
   - If you wrapped the stone in cloth, dunk the wrapped stone in hot, soapy water to wet it completely, squeeze the stone for about 5 minutes, remove the cloth and continue to press in on the stone until the wool fits tightly with no wrinkles. (This is the same technique used for adding the outside layer to the felt ball; see page 76.)
   - If you haven't wrapped or tied the wool, hold the wool tightly to the stone as you wet it with hot, soapy water. Press straight into the stone for several minutes until the wool shrinks and becomes smooth.
4. When the wool has felted and shrunk to form a smooth surface, rub the stone all around on the washboard or another bumpy surface. Rinse at intervals, and check for soft areas. Then add more soapy water or soap your hands with bar soap, and continue to press and rub the wool. When the felt is tight around the stone, rinse out the soap, blot the piece in a towel, and let it dry.

5. For best results, allow the felt to dry completely before opening the vessel. Decide how you want the vessel to open. (Note that the opening of the vessel has to be big enough to allow the widest part of the stone to go through without stretching the felt.) Cut around the stone using a sharp blade (photo 5), remove the stone (photo 6), then use sharp pointed scissors to snip any stray fibers.

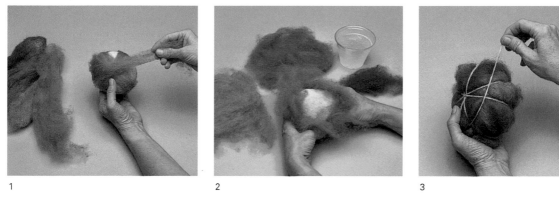

1   2   3

  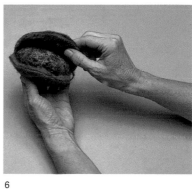

4   5   6

An uncut felted stone and three round vessels with the stones removed.

Vessel Ideas

You can make a variety of vessels by covering different-shaped stones or other hard objects, and you can make square or rectangular vessels by covering boxes instead of stones.

FELT BOXES

Lovely felt boxes for your own jewelry or for gifts can be made by covering blocks or plastic boxes with wool and then felting them (**photos 1 and 2**).

1

2

FELT EGG WITH BABY DUCK INSIDE

Make a felt egg by wrapping white wool around a plastic Easter egg, an oval stone, or a Styrofoam egg covered with plastic wrap (**photo 3**), and put a felt duckling inside (see page 49 for an example of a felt duck).

MEDICINE POUCH NECKLACE

Medicine pouch necklaces can be made by felting around a flat stone and cutting an opening only at one end (**photo 4**).

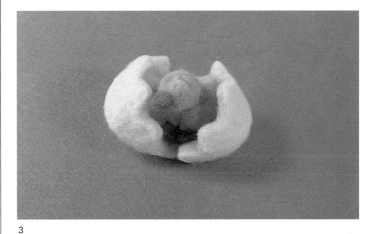

3

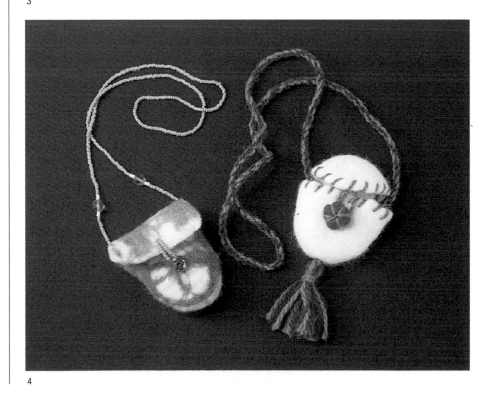

4

10
Seamless Wearables

Felt wearables are attractive and practical, offering the warmth and softness of wool and excellent durability. The basic technique for creating seamless felt wearables is the same whether you are making a hat with ear flaps, a rolled-brim hat, aprés-ski boots, slippers, or mittens.

The Scandinavian Feltmaking Technique

The Scandinavian feltmaking technique for making a seamless slipper, hat, or mitten is similar to the procedure for making a seamless vessel. However, instead of wrapping the wool around a solid three-dimensional object, you use a flat pattern made of cloth, plastic, or other material that won't deteriorate when soaked with soapy water.

Most of the projects described in this book will succeed no matter what type of wool you are using. But to use the Scandinavian feltmaking technique to best advantage, you need to work with wool that felts quickly and easily. Before beginning any of the projects described here, check the end-of-book list of sources for wool for seamless wearables (page 140).

When figuring out how much wool you will need for your project, remember that you must allow for shrinkage: the pattern has to be larger than the desired finished size of the article. The felt may shrink by as little as 25 percent or as much as 50 percent, depending on the type of wool, the thickness of the batts, and the felting technique used. For each slipper, mitten, or hat, two felting batts are needed; each batt needs to be 2 to 3 inches larger than the pattern.

After cutting your pattern, you envelop it in wool using hot, soapy water, and felt the wool around the pattern. The pattern is removed before final felting and finishing. With this technique, it is not necessary to complete the felt project in one session. You can make a partially finished felt piece, allow it to dry, and return to finish the project at any time you desire.

The best way to learn the Scandinavian feltmaking method is to start with relatively uncomplicated wearables, such as child-size slippers or a teddy bear beret. Smaller pieces take less time to felt, and once you have mastered the basic technique, you can go on to more ambitious projects.

These seamless felt hats, slippers, and mittens were made using the Scandinavian feltmaking technique.

Slippers

WHAT YOU'LL NEED

Wool fleece, washed and carded

Pencil and paper

Material for a pattern (preferably a different color from the wool)

Hot soap-and-water solution

Washboard or other bumpy surface

Scissors

Towel

TIP: MAKING PATTERNS

This tip comes from fiber artist Pat Spark: Make your pattern out of paperboard (for example, oaktag or old cereal boxes), cover it with contact paper, and cover the edges with duct tape. It is easy to feel where such a thick pattern is inside the wool. When the felt shrinks to the point at which the pattern starts to buckle, it's time to remove the pattern and finish the felting.

Felt slippers are wonderfully warm, and if you make them thick enough, they will last a long time. Estimate the amount of wool you will need to make a pair of slippers using the following table:

Adult woman	4 to 5 ounces
Adult man	6 to 7 ounces
Child (1 to 4 years)	2 to 3 ounces
Child (5 to 10 years)	3 to 4 ounces

MAKING THE PATTERN

1. Trace your foot on a large piece of paper (**drawing 1**).
2. Make an oval around the tracing about 1 inch away from the edge.
3. Cut out the oval pattern (**photo 2**), tape it onto your pattern material, and cut out the pattern (**photo 3**). Be sure to save your paper pattern. You will need it later.

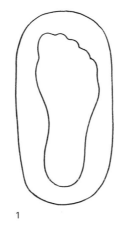

1

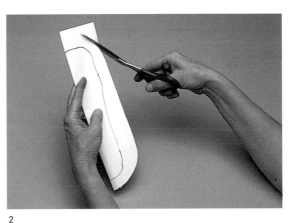

2

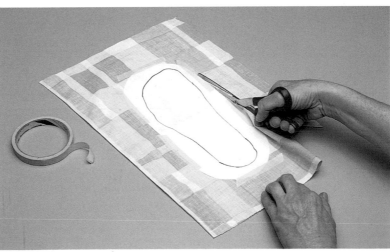

3

MAKING THE BATTS

4. Determine the total amount of wool you need for the slippers. (Use the table on page 107 as a guide. For thicker felt, use the next largest amount.)

5. Weigh out the amount of wool you will need for the batts and divide it into four equal piles. (You will be making four batts, two for each slipper.) Weigh out an extra ounce and keep it handy.

6. Make the batts one at a time from the four piles of wool. Following the instructions for layering a batt on pages 57–58, build each batt over the pattern, letting it extend 2 inches out from the pattern edge (photo 4). Each batt should have at least three layers. Keep layering the wool until you have used all the wool in that pile, then make the next batt. The batts should be as close to equal in size as possible.

7. Once your batts are completed, you can add color by placing dyed wool on top of two of the felting batts and use those batts as the outside or second batts for each slipper.

WETTING BOTH SIDES OF THE WOOL

8. Center the pattern over the first batt. For a plastic pattern, lift the pattern and pour about ⅛ cup of hot, soapy water into the center of the wool batt. For a cloth pattern, pour the water on top of it (photo 5), then wet down all of the wool underneath it by pressing down on it. Keep the wool that extends beyond the sides of the pattern dry.

9. When the wool under the whole pattern is lying flat, fold the dry wool around the outside of the pattern over the pattern right at the pattern edge (photo 6). If there is an area in the center where the pattern is not covered, take some wool from the ounce that you have set aside and cover the space. There should be an even thickness of wool covering the pattern.

10. Wet the wool down just enough for it to hold the shape of the pattern before you add the second batt (photo 7).

11. Sponge up any water around the slipper; then center the second batt over the slipper shape (photo 8). If you have used colored wool for the top layer, place the batt with the dyed side facing up.

12. Pour a small amount of hot, soapy water over the center of the batt directly over the pattern. Pat down the wool on top of the pattern, using more water if needed (photo 9).

13. When the wool over the pattern has been wet down, carefully pick up the project at the top and turn it over (photo 10).

14. Fold the dry wool back over the edges, as you did with the first batt (photo 11). If you want dyed wool on both the top and bottom of the slipper, place more dyed wool on top of the side now facing up before wetting down the wool.

   Your wool is now in the shape of a slipper, but the fibers are not felted together and they can easily be pulled apart. The next step is to felt the wool until it has shrunk and hardened enough to be cut into.

4

5

6

7

8

9

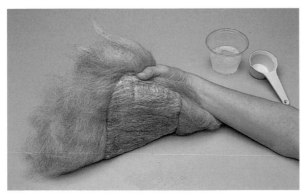

10

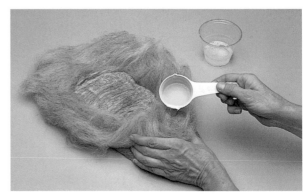

11

FELTING THE WOOL

As you apply pressure to your slipper during the next series of steps, you will be able to feel the difference in the material as the wool fibers bond. You will work first on one side of the slipper, and then the other. It usually takes 15 to 20 minutes for the wool to felt enough for you to go on to the final stage, although it may take longer. It may be helpful at this point to review the tips for applying pressure given in the bulleted list on page 60.

15. Press down on the wool-covered pattern with your fingertips for about 3 minutes, then use your whole hand. Use a strong even pressure, but do not press on the edges (photo 12).

16. When you feel the wool flattening under your hand and beginning to lose its softness, turn your project over and repeat the procedure. Again, be sure not to press on the edges.

17. If the fibers do not seem to be flattening and hardening, you can add more warm, soapy water. If the wool gets very sudsy, pour clear, warm water over the project and drain off the suds.

18. Turn the project back to the first side, and continue to apply pressure with your whole hand. As the fibers felt, gradually increase the pressure. Press each side thoroughly several times.

    After 15 to 20 minutes, your piece should hold its shape well enough and be firm enough for you to cut into, to open the slipper. (The piece will still be relatively soft.)

12

OPENING THE SLIPPER

19. Decide which side is the top of the slipper before you start to cut.

20. Check the size of the slipper by laying your paper pattern on top of it. Don't worry if the slipper is now bigger than the pattern; you will be able to shrink it on the washboard.
    - *If the slipper is close to the pattern size,* cut into the top, about one-fourth of the way in from the heel.
    - *If the slipper is bigger than the pattern,* center the paper pattern over the slipper, decide where you would cut on the paper pattern, and cut directly under that spot into the slipper.

21. With a pair of sharp scissors, cut straight down into the wool until you reach the cloth pattern (**photo 13**). Be careful not to cut through the pattern.

22. When you have cut a small hole, push up on the top layer from inside the slipper. Then place your scissors in the hole and cut toward the toe of the slipper, making a slit about the length of the four knuckles on your hand (**photo 14**). (For a child's slipper, you would cut a smaller slit.)

23. Rub the cut edges between your fingers to felt them so they won't stretch out (**photo 15**).

24. It is now time to felt the edges or seam area of the slippers. Place one hand inside the slipper, palm up, and turn the slipper so part of the seam is over your palm. Press on the seam with your outside hand against your hand inside the slipper, moving your hand back and forth about 1 inch (**photo 16**). Repeat this action all around the seam.

25. Remove the pattern and felt the inside of the slipper the same way, rubbing over the whole slipper.

26. Rinse the slipper in warm water and check the size.

    - If you can see that the slipper is nearly the right size, put it on. If it fits, you can work the felt with your hands, with the slipper on, to full and shape the felt, then go to Step 28 (page 113).

    - If it is much too big, don't worry. It will shrink during the fulling stage. Cut a larger opening if necessary, and decide which areas need shrinking or shaping.

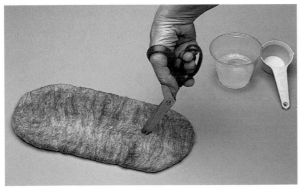

13

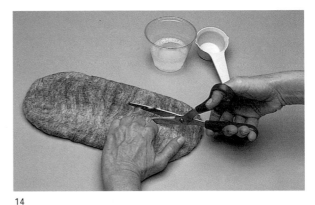

14

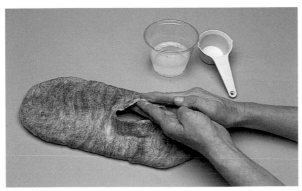

15

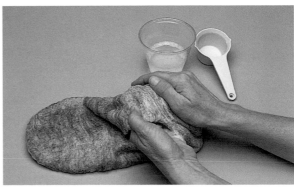

16

Fulling Felt for Wearables

The longer you full the felt, the more it will shrink and harden. It is easy to shrink a project too much, so check for size often. Work over your entire project, gradually working it with more pressure, rather than working one area for a long time.

1. First rinse your project and squeeze out as much water as you can.
2. Lay your project down on the washboard and add hot, soapy water to the area that you are working on.
3. Place your hand palm down inside the project, push down against the washboard, and rub the felt on the washboard.
4. Gently move the felt back and forth across the ridges of the washboard in short ¼-inch to ½-inch strokes.
5. As the felt hardens, increase the pressure and make your strokes longer. The wool will shrink in the direction you rub. Rub the toe and heel areas in a circular motion to toughen the felt and shape those areas.

When you are felting a wearable, it will shrink in the direction that you are rubbing. To shrink its length, rub it lengthwise on the washboard; to shrink its width, rub it sideways.

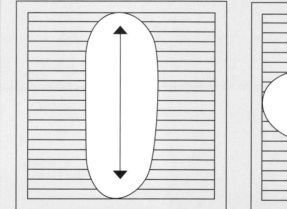

SHRINKS LENGTH OF SLIPPER

SHRINKS WIDTH OF SLIPPER

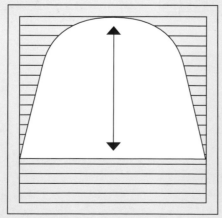

SHRINKS HEIGHT OF HAT

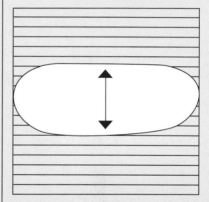

SHRINKS WIDTH OF HAT

FULLING AND DRYING THE FELT

27. Full your slipper, shrinking, hardening, and shaping the felt (**photos 17 and 18**). (See the box, "Fulling Felt for Wearables," on the opposite page.)

28. When the slipper has shrunk to the correct size and the wool is as smooth as you want it to be, rinse it and blot it dry in a towel (**photo 19**). Then shape it and let it dry (**photo 20**). The felt will not shrink any more as it dries.

17

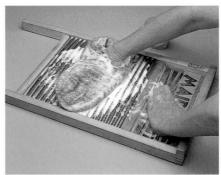

18

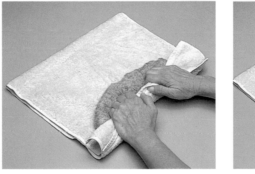

19

20

TROUBLESHOOTING

- *If your slippers are too big after you have worked them for a long time,* rinse your project in warm water, squeeze out as much soap and water as you can, add fresh soapy water as hot as you can comfortably stand, and rub the felt on the washboard using a lot of pressure. Turn the slipper inside out and rub it on the washboard.

- *If the felt is not smooth, but has flaps of wool,* add hot, soapy water to the flaps and gently rub them. Do not cut them off until you have finished felting and fulling and the project is almost the correct size. Then trim as needed and rub the cut areas. Turn the project inside out when you rub it on the washboard so that you are not rubbing those areas directly on the washboard. If you have made a very uneven felt, turn the project inside out and have the inside be the outside!

COMPLETING THE SLIPPERS

29. Using the same pattern, make the second slipper.
30. When the slippers are completely dry, you can make cords to sew around the openings (see the instructions on page 93). Using button-hole thread and a leather needle, you can also sew suede soles onto the bottoms of the slippers (see page 13 for an example).

A collection of warm, soft, felt slippers.

Mittens

WHAT YOU'LL NEED

Wool fleece, washed and carded

Pencil and paper

Material for a pattern (preferably a different color from the wool)

Mitten pattern (page 137)

Hot soap-and-water solution

Washboard or other bumpy surface

Scissors

Towel

Mittens can be made in the same way as the slippers. You start with a pattern in the shape of a mitten and envelop it in wool. When the pattern is being enveloped in wool, fold some extra wool around the pattern in the area between the thumb and fingers. When buying wool, use the following guide for quantity:

Adult mittens	3 ounces
Children's mittens	1.5 to 2 ounces

1. Use the pattern provided (page 137) or make a pattern by tracing around your hand on a large piece of paper. Make an even line around the tracing about 1 inch away from the line. Make the line $1/2$ inch away around the thumb.
2. Cut out a pattern in cloth or plastic.
3. Layer four batts using the pattern as a guide. Let the wool extend about 2 inches out from the edge of the pattern.
4. Place the pattern on top of the first batt and wet the wool under the pattern (**photo 1**). Fold the dry wool over the pattern and add extra wool where it doesn't cover in the middle of the mitten and at the corner between the thumb and fingers (**photo 2**).

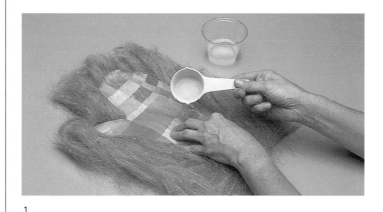

1

2

115

5. Lay the second batt on top of the pattern and wet the wool over the pattern. To incorporate color into the mitten, place dyed wool on top of this second batt (**photo 3**).

6. Felt the mitten, following the instructions for felting slippers (page 110). When the felt holds its shape well, you are ready to cut into the mitten.

7. Lay the mitten on a flat surface with the end to cut toward you. Carefully cut into the felt about 1 inch from one corner. When you find the pattern, insert the scissors and make a straight cut along the bottom edge to $1/4$ inch from each corner.

8. Felt the cut edge by pressing and rubbing it between your hands so it won't stretch out.

9. Work on the whole mitten inside and out. When the felt is strong enough, rub it on a washboard to shrink and shape it (**photo 4**).

3

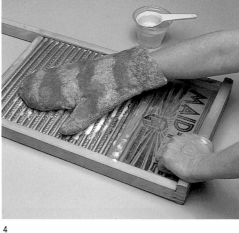

4

A finished pair of multicolored felt mittens.

Hats

WHAT YOU'LL NEED

Wool fleece, washed and carded

Pencil and paper

Material for a pattern (preferably a different color from the wool)

Basic hat pattern (page 138)

Hot soap-and-water solution

Washboard or other bumpy surface

Scissors

Towel

You can make a felt hat by following the technique for seamless wearables described for slippers and mittens. Using the basic hat pattern (page 138), you can create several styles of felt hat, including rolled-brim hats and hats with ear flaps. Use the following table to estimate how much wool you will need:

Child (1 to 4 years)	2 ounces
Child (5 to 10 years)	3 ounces
Adult woman	3 to 4 ounces
Adult man	4 to 5 ounces

MAKING THE PATTERN

1. Enlarge the hat pattern on a copying machine. For a child's hat, enlarge the pattern as indicated. For an adult size, after enlarging the pattern, increase the width of the pattern by 2 inches on each side.
2. Cut out the paper pattern, then cut out a pattern in cloth or plastic (photo 1).

MAKING THE BATTS

3. Using the table above, weigh out the amount of wool you will need and divide it into two equal piles.
4. Make two layered batts, following Steps 4 to 7 under "Slippers," page 108.

1

WETTING AND FELTING THE WOOL

5. Follow Steps 8 to 14, under "Slippers," page 108, until the felt is the right texture and shape to cut.

Making Turned Edges

If you make a turned edge on the hat following the steps below, you will not have to cut into the felt to open the hat. The opening of the hat can be made as you wet down the wool over the pattern.

- Wet the pattern down on top of the first batt (**photo 2**).
- Lift the pattern and fold the dry wool extending out from the edge of the pattern over the wet wool on the hat (**photo 3**).
- Replace the pattern and wet the wool down (**photo 4**).
- Do the same thing for the other side when you place the second batt over the pattern. Wet the wool to the edge of the pattern, then fold the dry wool onto the wet wool to make the edge of the hat.

2

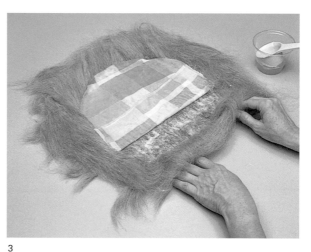

3

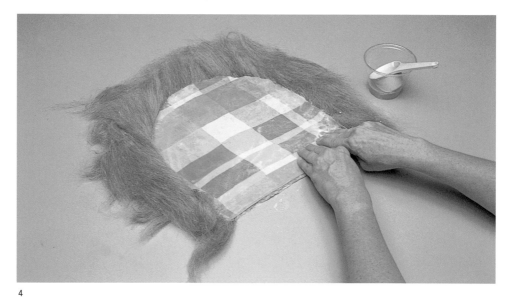

4

Opening the Hat

6. If you haven't made a turned edge on the hat opening, lay the hat on your work surface with the straight edge of the pattern shape toward you.

7. Poke the point of your scissors into the center of this edge a few inches from one corner. Make small snips in the wool to find the pattern.

8. When you find the pattern, push up on the top layer from the inside and cut along the edge to $1/4$ inch from each corner, then felt the cut edge by pressing and rubbing it with your fingers.

Felting the Cut Edge and the Seam

9. Felt the cut edge by pressing and rubbing it between your hands.

10. Now felt the uncut edges or seam of the hat, to make it as strong as the rest of the hat.
    - Place one hand inside the hat, palm up.
    - Turn the hat so part of the seam is over your palm.
    - Press on the seam with your outside hand against your hand inside the hat, moving your hand back and forth about an inch.
    - When that spot is smoothed out, repeat this action all along the seam, then all over the hat.

CHECKING THE SIZE

11. Dunk the hat in water, rinse out most of the soap, and blot it with a towel. The felt should hold together but still feel soft. At this point, you probably have a large, floppy hat as large or larger than your pattern.
    - If the hat is too big and floppy, shrink and harden the felt on the washboard, following the steps given in the Box "Fulling Felt for Wearables," on page 112. As you are fulling the hat, check for size often. The felt will shrink in the direction you are rubbing. Leave the hat a little large even after fulling because the hat will shrink further when you rinse it. After fulling, rinse the hat again.
    - If your hat holds its shape well and is the right size, you can go on to Step 12.

FINISHING THE HAT

12. Follow the instructions for "Rolled-Brim Hats" or "Hats with Ear Flaps," below.

13. Rinse the hat in clear water until all of the soap is out and squeeze out the excess water.

14. Dry the hat by blotting it in a clean towel.

15. If you have chosen the rolled-brim hat style, roll up the edges of the hat.

16. Shape the hat and allow it to dry in the shape you want.

17. Add any decorations or embellishments, such as embroidery or ties. (Instructions for making ties for hats are on page 93.)

Rolled-Brim Hats
- Trim the uneven edges of the hat if necessary.
- Rub and felt the cut edges of the hat, adding warm, soapy water as needed.

Hats with Ear Flaps
- Place the hat on your head and have someone draw around the hat with a water-based felt-tip marker where the edge of the hat should be.
- Take the hat off and check to make sure that the line is the same on both sides of the hat (that is, make sure it is symmetrical).
- Adjust the line as needed.
- When cutting, leave $1/2$ inch more felt than the line indicates. Cut around the hat $1/2$ inch outside the line (**photo 5**).
- Try the hat on again.
- After cutting, rub the felt and the cut edges of the hat. Add hot, soapy water as needed to felt and finish the edges and wash out the marker line. This felting will shrink up that extra $1/2$ inch that you left on when cutting.

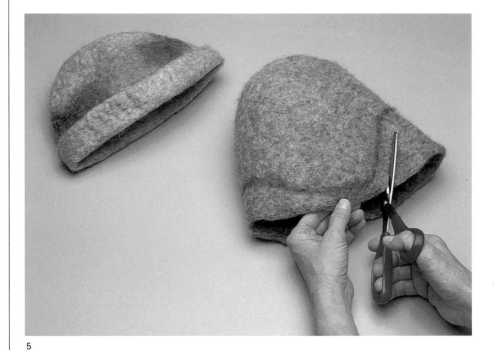

5

A rolled-brim hat.

This felt hat with earflaps incorporates a bright yellow embroidered sun.

A hat with earflaps. The edge design was embroidered with yarn and a tapestry needle.

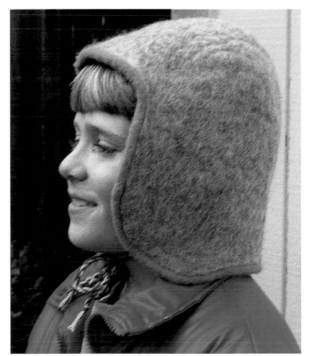

Hat with earflaps. The green edge was made by sewing a felt rope to the edge.

Teddy Bear Berets

WHAT YOU'LL NEED

1/8 to 1/4 ounce wool (enough for three layers in each batt)

Hot soap-and-water solution

Scissors

Pencil and paper

Material for a waterproof pattern

Another small project for the seamless wearable technique is a teddy bear or doll beret. After you have made a beret, make a matching flat piece of felt using the same wool fleece for a matching coat and hat set for a well-dressed bear.

1. Calculate the size your pattern should be. The beret pattern is a circle that is larger than the bear's head to allow for shrinkage of the felt. With a ruler, estimate the diameter of the teddy bear's head. Double the number. The doubled number will be the diameter of your pattern. For example, if you have a teddy bear with a 2-inch head, you will make a pattern with a diameter of 4 inches.

2. Cut out the pattern in a waterproof material (cloth, plastic, etc.).

3. Place your pattern on a flat surface and use it as a guide to layer two felting batts. Each batt should have three thin layers of wool with the fibers in each layer lying crosswise to the fibers in the adjacent layer.

4. Add color to the batt that will be the top of the beret (**photo 1**).

5. Prepare a hot, soapy water solution.

The next few steps are very similar to Steps 8 to 26, under "Slippers" (see pages 108–111).

6. Place the pattern on top of the first batt and wet down the wool beneath the pattern (**photo 2**).

7. Fold the dry wool extending out from the edge of the pattern over the pattern (**photo 3**).

8. Place the second batt over the pattern and wet down the wool that is lying directly over it, then turn the piece over and fold the wool over that side of the pattern. When the pattern is covered with wool, begin to felt the wool by pressing gently in the middle of the beret while avoiding the outside edge (**photo 4**). Turn it over and press on the other side. Work on each side for 3 to 5 minutes until you feel the wool in the middle of the piece turn to soft felt.

9. Decide which side you want for the top of the beret, then cut a slit in the opposite side down to the pattern (**photo 5**). Make the slit large enough to fit two or three fingers through. Be careful not to cut through the pattern. Press and rub the cut edges to prevent them from stretching out. Continue to felt the wool especially the outside edges that you avoided before.

10. After you have softly felted the entire beret, rinse it in clear, warm water and check it for size. Cut a 1/2 circle on each side of the slit to make the head opening. Then try the beret on the bear. If the beret needs more felting, you can rub it on a washboard to further shrink and shape it.

11. When the beret has shrunk to size to fit the bear, rinse it and squeeze out the water. Then let it dry flat.

1

2

3

4

5

You can dress your bear by making a flat piece of felt for a cape or shirt, cutting perpendicular slits in the middle for the bear's head.

A pair of stylishly bereted bears.

11
Puppets

You can make delightful finger puppets using wool and a wooden spoon, and you can make an amazing variety of hand puppets using the techniques for seamless wearables. You can sew or glue features onto your puppets, or use surface design techniques.

You can easily turn your puppet designs into stuffed toys by sewing up the openings. Wait until the felt is dry, then stuff the shape with clean fleece.

Finger Puppets

WHAT YOU'LL NEED

Combed or carded
wool fleece

Wooden spoon with a
thick round handle

Liquid soap or soap gel
(see page 24)

Hot soap-and-water
solution

Needle and thin yarn
(for embroidering
features) *or*

Thick thread (for tying
head off from body)

Glue

Towel

The simplest puppet is a finger puppet felted around the end of a wooden spoon.

1. Pull a couple of handfuls of fiber from the end of the roving or carded wool. Fold them over the end of the spoon. Hold them in place as you wrap fibers around the spoon to hold them (**photo 1**). Fold more wool over the end of the spoon and again hold them in place as you wrap more fibers around the spoon.
   - For a one-color puppet, keep wrapping until you have covered the bowl of the spoon with four to five layers of wool.
   - For a doll with clothes, wrap the top of one-half of the spoon with a skin color, then use another color for wrapping the lower part.
2. While holding the wool in place on the spoon, wet the wool with soap gel or squirt a few drops of liquid soap onto it. Use just enough water to mat down all of the wool without making it sudsy.
3. Press and squeeze the wool for 3 to 5 minutes until it fits tightly to the spoon without wrinkles (**photo 2**).
4. Rub the wool with your hands for a few more minutes, then rub it on a washboard or bumpy surface (**photo 3**).
5. Rinse the wool by dipping it in warm, clear water and squeezing it. Then slip the softly felted wool off of the spoon.
6. Continue to felt the puppet by adding hot, soapy water and rubbing it gently on a washboard, holding it with one or two fingers inside the puppet. Work the felt, gradually increasing the pressure, until the piece is nicely felted, then gently rinse the felt and blot it dry in a towel.
7. Stuff some dry wool into the puppet all the way to the end for the head, and tie a piece of heavy thread or yarn tightly around the felt about 1 inch from the end (**photo 4**). This will be the head of the puppet.
8. Finish the finger puppet by stitching eyes, nose, and mouth and gluing or sewing on hair. For animal puppets, make a piece of flat felt from the same material and cut out ears, then sew or glue them onto the puppet.

1

2

3

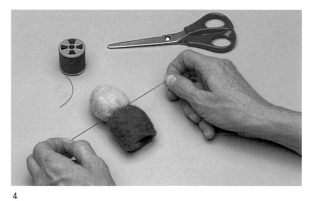

4

Finished finger puppets, with stitched and glued features.

Hand Puppets

WHAT YOU'LL NEED

Wool fleece, carded or combed, natural and/or dyed

Hot soap-and-water solution

Puppet pattern (page 139)

Plastic or cloth for the pattern

Washboard or other bumpy surface

Towel

To make hand puppets, you use the seamless wearable technique described on pages 106–114. You can also create a variety of embellishments for your puppets by using surface design techniques.

1. Enlarge the puppet pattern (page 139) and transfer it to a piece of cloth or plastic (**photo 1**).
2. Layer two felting batts, adding a design or extra color to one side of the second batt if desired.
3. Center your pattern on top of the first batt and wet down the wool underneath the pattern (**photo 2**). At the bottom edge of the puppet, fold the pattern back and fold the dry wool over the wet wool to make a turned edge. (The turned edge is to keep the felt from closing at the bottom, so you will not have to use scissors to open the puppet.)
4. Fold the dry wool extending out from the edge over the pattern.
5. At the four areas where the arms meet the body, fold extra wool around the pattern. Wet down the wool just to hold it in place (**photo 3**).
6. Center the second batt over the pattern. Wet down the wool that is directly over the pattern. At the bottom edge, again fold the dry wool back onto the wet wool to make the opening of the puppet.
7. Follow the directions for felting and fulling in Chapter 10, "Seamless Wearables," pages 110–113.
8. Rinse the puppet and let it dry.
9. Add ears and/or features (**photo 4**).

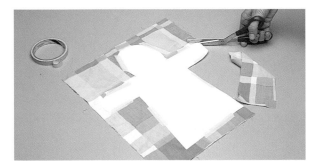

1

2

3

4

A finished bunny hand puppet. The bunny's ears are made from flat felt pieces and the eyes, nose, and whiskers are stitched.

A hand puppet tiger made in the same way the bunny was made.

Stuffed toys can be made by stuffing wool into a seamless puppet and stitching the opening closed. Or, make a seamless piece of felt using the toy pattern. Make an opening on the bottom for stuffing the toy and remove the pattern, then stitch the opening closed.

12
Making a Felt Scene

Using the basic feltmaking techniques covered in this book, you can create felt scenes with dwellings, people, and animals.

A Felt Scene with Poseable Figures

WHAT YOU'LL NEED

Wool in skin and clothing colors

Stretch elastic tube gauze (4-inch piece for each figure)

Sewing needle and thread

Pipe cleaners

Soap gel

This charming felt scene depicts a nomadic group arranged in front of a traditional yurt. The yurt was made of five pieces of flat felt laid over a bamboo and reed frame. It is 14 inches high and 16$^1/_2$ inches wide. The three women in the foreground are shown making felt using the rolling technique described on pages 68–69. The felt door flap on the yurt was made using the wet inlay technique outlined in the section on surface design.

POSEABLE FIGURES

To make the figures in the scene on the opposite page, felt colored wool around pipe cleaner skeletons. Create heads by stuffing gauze tubes with wool and then attaching them to the pipe cleaner bodies.

People

1. Make a pipe cleaner body. Wrap two pipe cleaners together to make a stronger frame.
2. Twist the piece of tube gauze in the middle and fold it in half (**photos 1 and 2**).
3. Push one half of the gauze into the other half. Now you have one tube with a double thickness of gauze (**photo 3**).
4. Stuff wool into the tube for the head (**photo 4**).
5. Wrap thread around the head vertically and horizontally to make an indention at the eyes and the hairline. Stitch the threads together where they cross on either side of the head. Then push one side of the horizontal thread down to the neck.
6. Stitch around the bottom of the gauze packet to close it, then stitch the head onto the pipe cleaner figure.
7. Wrap wool around the figure to make the body (**photo 5**). First wrap skin colored wool for the head and hands (and legs for girls) and a dark color for shoes at the feet. Then use clothing colors for the rest of the doll. Wrap the wool firmly and evenly.
8. Use soap gel and a little hot water to massage the wool, felting it.
9. Rinse the figure and let it dry.
10. After the figures have dried, sew on hair.

Camels

1. Wrap wool around a skeleton shape of the figure made from pipe cleaners to form the body.
2. Felt the outside layer of wool to form a felt skin.

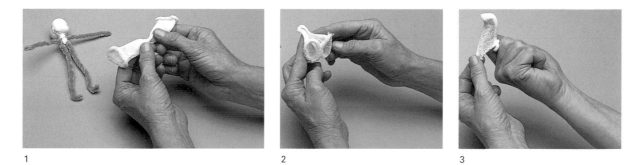

1   2   3

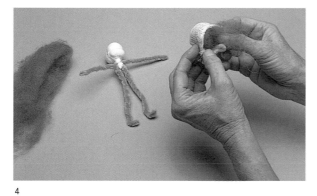

4   5

The design of the figures and camel in this lovely felt scene are by Fe Langdon for Waldorf School of the Peninsula.

Patterns

When making a felting pattern, the first step is to copy the one you want to use. By using a photocopier with an enlargement/reduction feature, you can simultaneously copy the pattern and enlarge or reduce it to the desired or required size. Simply enter the percentage for enlargement or reduction into the photocopier, then copy the pattern from this book.

If you would prefer to use the pattern at another size than what is indicated, or if no specific instructions accompany the pattern, you can use a calculator to compute the percentage for reduction or enlargement by dividing the intended pattern size by its current size.

- *Example 1: Enlarging.* If the pattern is 6 inches wide and needs to be $9\frac{1}{2}$ inches wide, you must enlarge it 1.58 times its current size ($9.5 \div 6 = 1.58$), or enlarge it at 158 percent.
- *Example 2: Reducing.* If the pattern is 6 inches wide and needs to be $4\frac{1}{2}$ inches wide, you must reduce it 0.75 times its current size ($4.5 \div 6 = 0.75$), or reduce it at 75 percent.

FLOWER PETALS

Enlarge or reduce as desired, or use at same size. See page 65 for project instructions.

BUTTERFLY WINGS

Enlarge or reduce as desired, or use at same size. See page 87 for project instructions.

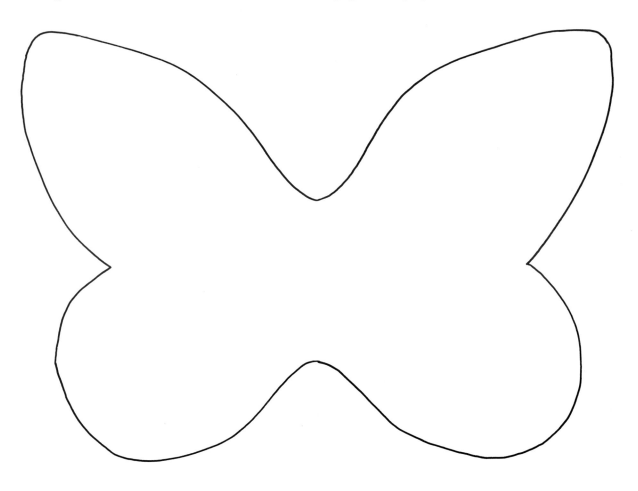

MITTEN
Enlarge 167%. See pages 115–116 for project instructions.

HAT

Enlarge 222%. See pages 117–121 for project instructions.

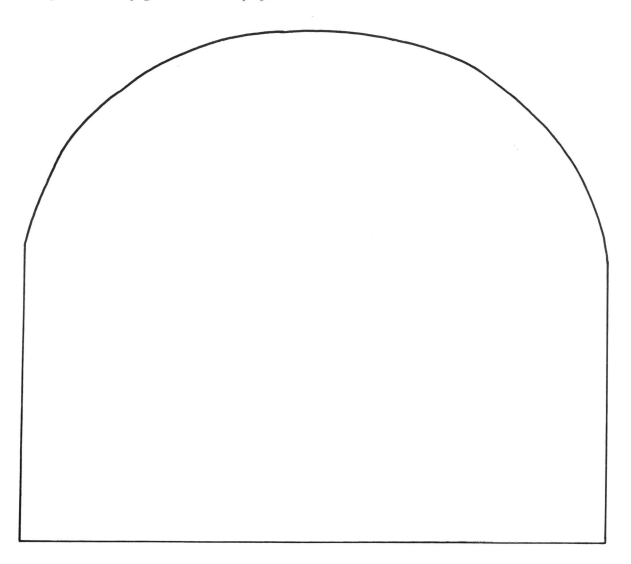

HAND PUPPET

Enlarge 222%. See pages 128–129 for project instructions.

Source Directory

Listed below are manufacturers, wholesalers, and mail order suppliers of different types of wool, feltmaking supplies, books, kits, and other felt-related materials. In some cases you can order directly from a source; in others, you will be provided with a list of retail distributors in your area.

Craft stores and shops that carry supplies for handweaving usually carry carded wool. In craft stores, carded wool is often in the doll supplies section, where it is sold as doll hair. If a local retailer doesn't have what you need, they may be willing to order it for you.

If you live near a sheep-farming region, you may be able to purchase raw fleece from a local farmer. Local county extension agents can give you a list of wool growers' associations and contacts.

WOOL

Bullen's Wullen's
5711 CR #13
Centerburg, Ohio 43011
(800) 565-7290
Wool roving

Donna Gallagher
Creative NeedleArts, Inc.
P.O. Box 415
Westerville, Ohio 43081
(614) 895-1017
FAX (614) 895-3525
Wool roving

Halcyon Yarn
12 School Street
Bath, Maine 04530
(800) 341-0282
Carded wool

Harrisville Designs
P.O. Box 806
Harrisville, New Hampshire
03450
(603) 827-3333
Carded wool

Norsk Fjord Fiber
P.O. Box 271
Lexington, Georgia 30648
(706) 743-5120
Wool fleece and carded wool imported from Scandinavia

Wilde Yarns
3737 Main Street
P.O. Box 4662
Philadelphia, Pennsylvania
19127-0662
(215) 482-8800
Carded wool and yarn

WOOL AND OTHER FELTMAKING SUPPLIES

Columbus Washboard Co., Inc.
1372 Oxley Road
Columbus, Ohio 43212
(800) 343-7967
Manufacturer of washboards

FeltCrafts
P.O. Box 426
Geneva, New York 14456
(800) 450-2723
Metal washboards, books, videos, and feltmaking kits

Peace Fleece
RR1, Box 57
Kezar Falls, Maine 04047
(800) 482-2841
E-mail: saw@igc.apc.org
Carded wool and feltmaking kits

Woodland Woolworks
262 South Maple
P.O. Box 400
Yamhill, Oregon 97148
(800) 547-3725
Wool, washboards, and felting boards

ORGANIZATIONS

International Feltmakers
Association
Isell Hall
Cockermouth
Cumbria, UK CA13 0QC

North American Felter's Network
1032 SW Washington Street
Albany, Oregon 97321
(541) 926-1095
Members receive an informative quarterly newsletter

PUBLICATIONS
The following publications, which focus primarily on weaving, sewing, and related fiber arts, occasionally feature feltmaking techniques and projects.

FiberArts Magazine
Altamount Press, Inc.
50 College Street
Asheville, North Carolina 28801
(704) 253-0467
FAX (704) 253-7952

Handwoven and *Spin Off*
Interweave Press
201 East Fourth Street
Loveland, Colorado 80537
(970) 669-7672

Shuttle, Spindle & Dyepot
The Handweavers Guild of America
2 Executive Concourse
Suite 201
Duluth, Georgia 30136
(770) 495-7702

Threads
The Taunton Press
63 South Main Street
Newtown, Connecticut 06470
(203) 426-8171

Index